A ***POCKET GUIDE*** *FOR*

PROJECT MANAGERS

Maximize People, Process, and Tools

MICHAEL J. BETTIGOLE

A POCKET GUIDE FOR PROJECT MANAGERS
MAXIMIZE PEOPLE, PROCESS, AND TOOLS

iUniverse books may be ordered through booksellers or by contacting:

iUniverse
1663 Liberty Drive
Bloomington, IN 47403
www.iuniverse.com
1-800-Authors (1-800-288-4677)

ISBN: 978-1-4917-3199-4 (sc)
ISBN: 978-1-4917-3203-8 (hc)
ISBN: 978-1-4917-3202-1 (e)

Printed in the United States of America.

iUniverse rev. date: 09/23/2014

The support of my family permitted this labor of love to endure:

My wife, Kathy; her love and support never waivers.

My children, who make it all worthwhile.

My parents, who instilled the gift of commonsense wisdom.

Contents

Introduction

A Pocket Guide for Project Managers is a collection of strategies, maxims, and suggestions for anyone with the desire to become a better project manager or simply to become more effective as a leader. This book assumes you are a project manager today, wish to become one, or are responsible for developing leaders.

The advice here is not revolutionary. It is consistent with the multitude of theories, methodologies, and practices that are available and well documented under the subject of project management. This collection seeks to organize, in succinct fashion, the most effective pieces of wisdom and offer them as practical, real-world advice that anyone can apply immediately and with confidence.

An unattributed author once penned, "Good judgment comes from experience, and experience comes from bad judgment." The contents of this book were born from many, many instances of bad judgment and the opportunity to turn those circumstances into valuable experience. I once embarrassed a project participant for failing to produce his deliverables on time, but I didn't have all the facts and I was wrong. That was bad judgment, and I learned a lot from it. My hope is that you can too, because, like you, I experienced countless situations when managing projects that tested my ability to grow and turn mistakes into opportunities.

As a manager and leader in the financial services industry, I spent decades managing projects, building project management offices, developing tools, mentoring project managers, and remaining accountable for the successful delivery of multimillion-dollar initiatives. Sharing my experience and helping others learn from it is my motivation for writing this book.

Chapter one outlines the fundamental aspects of project management that contribute to project success and failure: accountability, communication, transparency, governance, control, leadership, and style, and tools. Each chapter then examines these topics in depth and offers case studies and real-life examples to demonstrate the concepts in action. The case studies and stories are real, with names and places changed for obvious reasons. These real-life examples are included to establish the connection between theory and practice and are intended to help illustrate what to do when something goes wrong.

You can choose to read straight through the material or take these points slowly, a few at a time, and in no particular order. Some have a multiperspective view of the most important aspects of leadership and project management. An American proverb says that action without thought is like shooting without aim. This is a reference guide intended to provide thought to the actions a project manager (or leader) may take. It is intended to help leaders stay a successful course and prevent the trappings that usually doom a project—or, worse, prevent a project manager from rising above the mediocre percentage who never distinguish themselves as anything but glorified coordinators.

A project manager (or portfolio manager or program manager or delivery manager) is a leader and therefore must adopt the universal qualities that all successful leaders share. Many of the adages here are common to general leadership advice, a theme that is intentional and natural given the responsibilities of anyone with the word *manager* in his or her job title.

Despite years of experience, despite the certifications you may hold and your mastery of the industry you work in, the odds are already against you before you start a new project. Many projects begin to fail, in one respect or another, before the project manager gets involved.

By reading this book and incorporating its advice, it is my desire that you can avoid the majority of problems that cause project managers, and thus their projects, to fail. I hope you will establish yourself as a confident leader with an arsenal of tactics that will help you consistently deliver success.

Michael J. Bettigole

Chapter One
The Problems that Cause Projects to Fail

My life has been largely spent in affairs that required organization. But organization itself, necessary as it is, is never sufficient to win a battle.
—Dwight D. Eisenhower

In many industries, including government, no matter what the economy is like, no matter how many hours are devoted, and no matter how bright the people on the team are, a certain percentage of projects will fail to realize the success of on-time, within-budget delivery. Many may terminate without reaching the (originally) intended goal.

What is it about all these ventures that causes such disappointing results?

I have studied the patterns and circumstances surrounding project success and failure for over twenty years, mostly in the financial services industry. I looked at big projects, small projects, global projects, multimillion-dollar projects, and mission-critical projects. What I found was a specific set of characteristics linking those undertakings that deliver on time, come in within budget, and achieve what's anticipated at the project's inception.

- *Accountability* among project team participants is essential.
- End-to-end *communication* must remain open and flow without extended downtime.
- Achieving a proper level of *transparency* for all levels of management is a must.
- A consistent *governance and compliance* model is key to repeatable success.
- Proper project *control* is always needed to provide early assistance to troubled areas.
- Active *leadership* is essential, combining an effective style with proven tactics to understand how to unlock the talent and expertise of the team in cohesive fashion.
- The right *tools* can make all the difference, but there is no silver bullet. Understanding how to employ the right toolset, including methodology, is a critical component to success.

Accountability

Accountability is maintaining responsibility for all aspects of delivery for a project, a program, or the effectiveness of a project management office. We all like to think that our team of professionals—most of whom carry impressive certifications—are and remain accountable to the mission, the sponsors, and the overall initiative. Most project management offices (PMOs) have little choice but to rely on said professionalism or on threats to ensure that everyone maintains their accountability.

The underlying reason for this lack of choice is that most project participants don't feel a sense of urgency to communicate their statuses. When and if they do, the updates are sanitized to ensure nothing is communicated or published that could reflect negatively on themselves or their group. There isn't a great conspiracy at work. It's human nature, but that doesn't remove the need to achieve the highest degree of accountability from all project team members throughout the life cycle.

Communication

Communication is conveying necessary information to needed parties at the right time and in a way that leaves little room for misunderstanding. Many years ago—and it may still hold true today—one of the two hundred questions on the Project Management Professional (PMP) exam was "Which percentage of a project manager's day is spent on communication?" *Ninety percent* was the correct answer.

When executing a project of any size or importance, it's difficult to overcommunicate to the project team. When everyone is aware of the big picture, knows what's going on, and feels connected to the decision makers, there is simply better participation and teamwork. However, when project members feel out of touch or out of the loop, productivity and morale suffer.

Most projects are managed through e-mail and spreadsheets. Ironically, many believe this is the very epitome of communication, when in fact these are some of the most inefficient methods to manage a project or a team. It is the project manager's job to ensure communication remains open and available to all the project participants. This includes access to appropriate documentation, such as the project plan and schedule, as well as meeting minutes and risk action plans. E-mail is a wonderful tool, but it does not replace the need for well-run meetings, a central repository for project documentation, and informal, personal interaction among project team members to share ideas.

Transparency

Transparency, in the context of project management, refers to the ability of project participants, including sponsors and stakeholders, to maintain awareness and understanding of project details (issues, risks, dependencies, and constraints) as the project is executed and circumstances change. Without adequate transparency into the day-to-day operations of a project, project managers are at a disadvantage. They are unable to monitor items closely enough to ensure corrective action is taken early, when it is needed most. Senior management, as well as sponsors and stakeholders, are also at a disadvantage because their reliance on the project manager to raise risks and issues is compromised. Most PMO staff react to issues and manifested risks because they did not have sufficient forewarning of developing issues to position the team to take proactive action.

The benefit of increased transparency is the ability to take corrective action early, when it has the best chance of positively impacting project results. No one enjoys reporting bad news, but as the adage says, bad news early is good news. PMO staff, stakeholders, and managers need a better strategy to ensure everyone has the necessary transparency, rather than hope project team members provide all the needed details in a timely manner.

Governance

Governance is sometimes a scary word. In this context, governance refers to a set of standard practices, procedures, rules, definitions, and nomenclature that everyone within a team, logical unit, business area, or organization agrees to adopt. The benefit of a governance model is standardization, which permits everyone to speak the same language across different businesses, departments, or geographical regions.

Project managers, especially the seasoned ones, are sometimes reluctant to adopt a new governance model for fear it will introduce different, untested tools or methodologies that offer nothing more than a lot of overhead and little assistance to get things done. Fair enough. Most governance models do seek to impose standards, but this doesn't mean governance is a bad thing.

When properly administered, a good governance model is as simple as standard values. For example, Green = No Issues, Red = Major Issues. A governance model allows different project managers to use different tools but maintain an agreed vocabulary that doesn't require translation from one project to another or one region to another. Setting up and documenting standards allows everyone, no matter their geographic location, to operate independently while knowing their process, methodology, vocabulary, and definitions are understood by all. A well-defined governance model allows project managers to take over different projects with seamless transition in shorter time periods, thus ultimately reducing overhead on training and knowledge transfer. A good governance model can help us move closer to that Holy Grail of doing more with less.

Control

Control is the ability of those in charge to take necessary action or make important decisions in order to provide course corrections when needed. It's not as daunting as it might sound. Sure, images of the PMO monster dictating policies and practices to the project managers may pop into your head when you think of project control, but this issue is much more subtle.

Every project is subject to ever-changing risks, scope creep, and issues that have potential to take matters in the wrong direction. It's the project manager's responsibility to present "actionable intelligence" to the appropriate people at the appropriate time. Maintaining control of a project requires the ability to drill down and spot problems before they become major issues.

The mantra "The higher you go, the fewer details are needed" highlights the need to be careful with the details you provide as you go up the chain of command. Senior leaders don't need to concern themselves with the nitty-gritty particulars of every task. However, if management doesn't have a mechanism to ensure accountability, transparency, and communication, supported by a proper governance model, then the ability to control a project is certainly lost.

Perhaps the most recent example of a project without adequate control was the failed launch of the Healthcare.gov website in October 2013. Despite the participation of talented people and a respected firm with plenty of experience, plus an impressive budget, the cross-functional project team lacked the necessary control to avoid a major disaster.

If a project manager does not know how to properly escalate problems to senior management, fails to understand the different types of escalation, and cannot determine when escalation is appropriate, then the ability of management to take necessary action at the proper time is further compromised. Knowing how, why, and when to escalate is fundamental to project control. There is more on proper forms of escalation in chapter six.

Leadership and Style

Leadership is the ability to create a vision, convince others that the vision is the right one, and coordinate disparate activities into a common cause through motivated commitment. I always imagine a project leader as a symphony conductor, responsible for making a wide breadth of instruments work together in harmony to produce pleasing music. A good leader knows how to coordinate the talents of many into harmonious collaboration. One's leadership *style* is a function of personality, experience, and mind-set.

Years of experience suggest that project managers are born and not made. Certainly, anyone can learn the essentials and practice the discipline to achieve a project manager position, and perhaps become very successful. However, not everyone can elevate the practice to new levels of effectiveness, efficiency, and leadership in a given organization. In the 1945 film *Rhapsody in Blue*, Oscar Levant, a contemporary and friend of George Gershwin, and a very accomplished musician himself, contrasted the early success of Mr. Gershwin with his own by saying they displayed the difference between genius and talent.

Project management requires a mixture of skill and talent. (Of course, genius doesn't hurt.) No matter how thoroughly you master project management methods, if you do not have the proper personality to deal with people, often at very chaotic times, then you will fail to coordinate them to act in harmony toward a common goal. Instincts play an important role when dealing with people, because so often the motivational factors that drive them and their behavior are already defined. The job of the project manager—or any leader, for that matter—is to uncover those motivational factors in order to create the best environment for individuals to succeed.

7

Every leader must develop his or her own management style, and that style is rooted in one's personality. There are many approaches and philosophies (McGregor's Theory X and Theory Y, Ouchi's Theory Z) that can assist with better and more effective management. The approach you choose, however, will have direct bearing on how people interact with you and whether or not they will take your call at five o'clock on a Friday.

There is a saying, "You can judge the character of a man by the size of the things that make him mad." This highlights the virtue of keeping focus on the most important things. Wisdom lies in knowing what to overlook and realizing that how you treat people is far more important than any project or deliverable.

Tools

There are quite literally thousands, if not millions, of project management tools available, and in most cases the right tool can make all the difference. Available in a variety of sizes, packages, and offerings, some are databases, some are calendars, some are task trackers, and some are collaboration portals, such as Microsoft's SharePoint.

With so many tools to choose from, selecting one that is appropriate, cost-effective, and accepted by the entire project team is often an intimidating task. Most tools come with the promise to erase organizational challenges, master scheduling, promote collaboration, open communication, and more. How do you pick from the plethora available? Are free tools less effective than those you pay for? Does success in one situation guarantee success in another?

Understanding how to evaluate project tools is the first step in selecting one that will help you prove to be a more effective project manager and leader. Fundamentally, there is no "right" or "wrong" tool. Tools are, rather, useful or not useful, and their usefulness can change as you move from project to project or from one organization to another.

Summary

The lack of accountability, communication, transparency, governance, control, and leadership are not the only problems that affect the success or failure of a project or a project manager. However, practice demonstrates that they remain at the top of the list.

Project teams often believe that sponsors are too disengaged from project execution and remain in ivory towers, unable to understand the trials the team must endure to make progress each day. There is a trickle-down effect of this belief that can manifest as disenchantment and a loss of alacrity. Addressing these problems with the right principles, values, and techniques, in any manner that works for your unique situation, will certainly add integrity to your efforts and usually result in delivery that is more successful.

The following pieces of advice were born from real-world situations spanning many, many years, extracted from many multimillion-dollar projects executed in Fortune 100 companies. They are based on observing people in different situations at different times in their careers, under wide-ranging circumstances, and applying age-old wisdom. In each case, the lessons learned helped deliver a more effectively managed project and distinguish individuals as leaders.

Chapter Two
Accountability

A leader is best when people barely know he exists.

—Lao Tzu

Accountability, in the context of project management, means maintaining responsibility for the delivery of a project and the effectiveness of a project management office. It also means being answerable to those who hired you and depend on you. It means you're in charge. The project relies on you and your management. Here are some tips for managing accountability.

1. A project manager must organize, centralize, communicate, and execute the details of a project in order to chart the course to successful delivery.

2. A project manager's job is not necessarily to do the work, but to make sure the work gets done. Project sponsors

and senior management rely on the project manager to be the single point of contact for all participants to ensure that work is completed. Coordination of the activities of different teams is part of a project manager's job description.

3. As project manager, you are responsible for everything that happens within the project. This means when things go wrong—and they will—you must accept responsibility and lead the recovery effort.

4. The project manager must do whatever is necessary to give each team member the greatest opportunity to accomplish his or her individual tasks. This means accepting a job description that might include things you have never associated with project management. At the end of the day, it is the project manager who assumes accountability for the outcome of the project, much like a captain on a ship. It is therefore essential that the project manager remain thoroughly engaged.

5. All projects suffer delays, setbacks, and problems. This is the reason a project manager is required. Unless the number of problems is egregious, a good project manager is not judged on the issues, but on how those issues are responded to. Therefore, it is critically important to remain accountable to the stakeholders and ensure that you accept ownership of the problems and their resolutions. When the San Francisco 49ers lost the Super Bowl to the Baltimore Ravens in February 2013, their quarterback, twenty-five-year-old Colin Kaepernick, said he made a lot of mistakes and reflected that *he* was not good enough. This is the epitome of a leader. Rather than blame his teammates or other circumstances that may have contributed, Kaepernick accepted the responsibility for the loss himself and moved on, saying, "It's good to get the experience."

6. Never assign an action item to more than one person or to someone who is not present. The assigned party must agree to accept ownership and the related responsibility of delivering.

7. If you attend a meeting via a conference bridge and announce yourself, you are committed to the meeting. You must stay for the entire meeting and pay attention to ensure that no one has a question or need for you. If you are on the agenda to provide an update, but must exit the meeting soon after, provide your update, ask if there are any questions, and, after dealing with those questions, announce that you are dropping from the call. Resist the temptation to multitask, relax your attention, or leave without announcing your premature exit.

This rule is centered on many, many experiences in which an otherwise successful meeting lost its value when critical members of the team dropped off an important call without notification. Not only was the accountability lost, but their conspicuous disrespect for the meeting chairperson left the other attendees wondering if there was sufficient reason to remain on the call.

Case Study: The Disappearing Caller

In one particularly embarrassing incident, Roger, a senior technology manager of a very large integration project between two companies, was required to provide a report on progress, issues, risks, and next steps each week via conference call. Each leader was allocated seven to ten minutes for an update. Since there were so many aspects of the project, from real estate to technology to human resources, the updates remained succinct and moved quickly.

After delivering his update and asking if there were any questions, Roger placed his phone on mute and moved on to other tasks. He kept the meeting on speaker at lowered volume, thinking he could monitor it in the background. Roger went about reading his e-mail and responding.

About thirty minutes later, another participant provided an update and had a question about a technology dependency. Since Roger wasn't listening attentively, he didn't hear the question or the context of the update. In fact, he didn't hear his name called out by several people, who were wondering if he was still on the call. The call ended with a promise to follow up with Roger after the meeting.

Later in the day, Roger was approached by the program manager—a woman he had tremendous respect and admiration for—and he realized what had happened. Not only was he embarrassed and disappointed about letting her down, but he soon learned that many on the call thought he was actively listening and simply didn't know the answer to the question. They thought he had pretended to be absent to avoid displaying his ignorance.

This bothered Roger even more. He knew his reputation was at risk, and worse, his character and integrity were called into doubt. It stunned him that his colleagues, some of whom he'd considered close, thought he would dodge a question rather than admit he didn't know the answer. For Roger it was far too high a price to pay, and he promised himself he would not get caught in such a situation again.

---

8. If you accept a meeting or schedule time with someone, honor your commitment. Don't cancel at the last minute; it demonstrates your loose command of time management and accountability. It may also leave your meeting party disappointed, perhaps the least desirable feeling you wish to have associated with you. However, sometimes things happen beyond your control, and you simply must cancel. In this case, take five minutes to sincerely apologize to your party through direct contact (not e-mail or text message). Avoid excuses and offer an alternative. Let the person know your true interest in meeting with him or her.

9. If you attend or chair a meeting, turn your phone off and don't constantly check it. Checking your phone demonstrates disrespect if it is perceived that you are mentally someplace else and not fully participating in the meeting. If you can't pay attention, how do you expect others to do so?

10. Always arrive to a meeting, especially one that you chair, a few minutes early, and hang around a few minutes after it concludes. This provides people an opportunity to speak off the record; some of the best project information comes in this manner.

11. Many reports use the common assessment rating scale known as RAG (red/amber/green) to illustrate the overall health of a project or deliverable. When you are using a RAG scale, a red or amber rating should not be viewed

as punitive. It is an opportunity for a project manager to highlight to management or stakeholders a need for corrective action. The key to using RAG ratings is making certain you have the entire set of facts that management will need in order to truly understand the project's health and make the necessary decisions. When advising your team, make certain this view of the ratings is clear to everyone working with you. Otherwise, you may receive status reports with RAG ratings that misrepresent the actual state of the project. Until you know your project team well, you can't take for granted their RAG ratings. Inspect each rating on its own merit; don't assume green is really green.

12.   Arrive at work early, before your manager. A good project manager should endeavor to always hear the news, good and bad, before his or her direct manager. If your boss tells you about a problem affecting your project that you should have been aware of but are not, you have failed a key accountability test. When managing a global project or program, make certain to enlist the help of your team members and stakeholders in other geographical regions to ensure that you are kept abreast of important news, especially if it occurs outside of your office hours.

13.   Reading this book suggests you want to improve your abilities, which means you likely enjoy what you do. In such a case, keep in mind that if you are forced to work with people who don't know what they are doing, especially other project managers, consider it your responsibility to teach them the right way. A good leader knows the importance of creating future leaders. That translates into making people more effective every day. Effectiveness is measured by the situation, but a project manager is almost always valued by the abilities to make progress, keep people informed,

create a sense of team, and bring calm to a situation. At the end of the day, critics will ask if the necessary things got done. Your ability to get more things done is a direct reflection on your leadership capabilities. Only insecure people feel the need to "protect" their successful tactics and methodologies.

14. No matter how good you are, at one point or another you will need help. A good project manager knows when to ask for help and how to ask for it. The first step, of course, is admitting to yourself that you need help and summoning the courage to seek it. When you do, make sure the person you approach is capable of solving your problem or can point you in the right direction. Research your position and options before you present to anyone. Prepare yourself for questions that may come your way. Seeking help in an appropriate fashion is a demonstration of control and accountability. Asking for help takes practice. If you need help and fail to ask for it, you can blame no one but yourself for the consequences. Learn to accept assistance when it is needed and to accept it with grace and humility.

15. One interpretation of the term *Superman complex* is a harmful sense of responsibility and/or the belief that everyone else on the team lacks the ability to successfully execute their tasks. In this context, someone with a Superman complex will approach his or her duties with the strong need to "save" others and take on most of the work solo. Project managers must avoid the Superman complex, lest they find themselves alienating their teams and creating disharmony, not to mention biting off more than they can honestly chew. It is good tonic to limit your area of involvement to no more than the number of projects or programs that you can remain sufficiently on top of within a ten-hour day. A valued project manager is the

axis of information for a select group of initiatives. Your value doesn't rise with the number of initiatives you take on. In fact, your value will diminish, because there is only so much information you can maintain mastery of. Avoid the temptation to fake it or exhibit heroics; it will catch up to you eventually.

16. To remain accountable and accessible, put your name and contact information on anything you publish. If you are reluctant to publish meeting minutes, status reports, articles, or position papers with your name and contact information, it's a good indication that you are not confident in the material or secure in representing it as your own. As the old adage says, if you want to sell something to someone, sell it to yourself first. Do not neglect to give credit where it is due. Use attribution as a tool to promote a team member or highlight a job well done. The team member will relish the credit, and it may even inspire sustained loyalty to you or the project.

17. Occasionally remind team members to review project material, and help them to do so. It is everyone's responsibility to remain familiar with the project plan, especially as it evolves, to ensure that they operate under the same knowledge of assumptions, risks, constraints, and approach. Unfortunately, most project participants don't keep abreast of the evolving plan of their own accord. Therefore, it is your responsibility as the project manager to help everyone be accountable and eliminate excuses, such as "I wasn't aware." Use your status meetings to highlight significant changes to the project plan.

18. Remind your team members that they can delegate their tasks to any number of people but that they maintain ownership of everything they delegate. When delegating,

give away the power along with the job, but retain the accountability.

Character, in many ways, is everything in leadership. It is made up of many things, but I would say character is really integrity. When you delegate something to a subordinate, for example, it is absolutely your responsibility and he must understand this. You as a leader must take complete responsibility for what the subordinate does. I once said, as a sort of wisecrack, that leadership consists of nothing but taking responsibility for everything that goes wrong and giving your subordinates credit for everything that goes well.

—Dwight David Eisenhower

19. There are countless variations of a status report. Each organization has a unique style and purpose. You may feel very comfortable with your version of a report, or believe it adds more value than other formats you are asked to produce, but resist the temptation to force a report format on your stakeholders. Rather, ask your audience what they want out of the report and how they will use it. Tailor the formatting and work hand in hand with your audience to maximize the value you give them. It's quite likely you will need multiple status report formats that convey the same message, so structure your information so you can use it across formats.

20. Once you create a report, put yourself in the position of the audience and ask what they would conclude based on your information as you have presented it. You may be surprised to discover that the information that makes perfect sense to you does not appear as clear to the target reader. Use a

critical eye to make necessary adjustments that ensure your intended message is delivered without ambiguity and in proper context.

21. A Turkish proverb advises one to turn around when one has gone the wrong way, no matter how far down the wrong road one has traveled. Immediately admit when you recognize you have made a mistake, even in the face of disgrace, and take corrective action, no matter how embarrassing it may seem and no matter how far down the road you are. It is impossible to be correct all the time. The sooner you realize this, the more effective you become at recognizing your mistakes and those of others. Once you identify a mistake, follow through with earnest confidence. If you are assisting another with correcting a mistake, do so quietly and without making the person feel foolish. This will pay dividends down the road.

22. The one who controls the message controls perception. Every project or major initiative is littered with rumors, speculation, and misinformation. You must endeavor to remain above the fray and be the source of accurate, up-to-the-minute information that all teams can rely on. Know the difference between news and gossip.

Case Study: The Inside Track

During the implementation of a technology project at a large, privately held institution, Tom, the project manager, found himself with the opportunity to meet one-on-one with the project's senior sponsor, Jon, to provide a briefing. Usually, Jon gathered his upper management once a month to update him on the various initiatives. It was August, and many people were on holiday. None of the senior managers were available for the August briefing, but Jon wanted to go ahead with it anyway.

Tom's boss, Peter, knowing his project was well under control with no significant risk of derailment, asked Tom if he wanted to conduct the briefing in Peter's stead. Tom jumped at the chance. In preparation, he updated his status reports, polished his language describing achievements and next steps, and became well versed in the status of dependent projects that could affect his. When he met with Jon, Tom was quite confident and feeling good.

"How's the team?" Jon asked. "How are they all doing?"

"Oh, all clear. They're fine," Tom replied briefly.

"C'mon. I know these guys are working nights and weekends, and that's on top of their day jobs. How are they really doing?" Jon pressed.

Tom hadn't prepared for this. He felt he had two choices: (1) maintain his positive, yet general statement, which was safe, but would certainly disappoint Jon, or (2) offer a few tidbits of rumored information, off the record, to demonstrate his depth of involvement with the team. The second option might even earn him points with Jon and get him invited back for more briefings.

"Well, this is unofficial," Tom replied and then chose to share some gossip about team members who were looking for new jobs because they had no faith management would adequately reward them at bonus time.

Jon was quite surprised and interpreted the message as the entire team's lack of faith surrounding management's ability to reward them. Correctly interpreting the surprise on Jon's face, Tom attempted to backpedal, but it was too late. The bell had been rung.

Fearing that a negative impression might be made on the broader teams, Jon met with his management team and directly addressed the issue of an unhappy work force. He emphasized the need to mitigate the risk of talent loss and, of course, the negative, unjust reflection on him. The management team was caught off guard and was a bit shocked. Eventually, the source of the information was discovered, and both Tom and his boss suffered a significant hit to their credibility.

Analysis:

Tom mistakenly thought he could score points by providing inside information to a senior sponsor, who he knew would never have insight into such issues. The information Tom provided was based on gossip that was perhaps true in isolated cases, but certainly not to the extent that required senior management to place mitigation around the risk. Tom made the mistake of trying to ingratiate himself with a senior sponsor, and wound up sending an alarming message that had unintended consequences for him and his boss.

Lesson:

Scoring cheap points with management rarely pays off in the long run. As the central source of information for your project, facts are your currency. If you begin trading in rumor or gossip, your currency will lose value, as will your credibility and effectiveness. Always stick to the facts.

---

23. Your project team needs to know the purpose of decisions and how they are made. If not, team members will act like robots and never alert you or others to potential risks. A good way to achieve a sense of team is to create a team identity, such as a website or a team logo, and make sure everyone connected to your project feels like part of it. Consider arranging exciting team-building exercises like a softball game, a bowling tournament for charity, or a hike. Everyone enjoys winning and will go above and beyond the call of duty if they feel like they are on the winning team. It's a powerful phenomenon that is often overlooked.

24. There are three cornerstones of trust that lead to accountability:

    a. A *depth of mutual respect* that allows team members to rely on each other

    b. The *ability and climate to speak candidly*, especially when things are not going so well

    c. The *confidence that others on the team will deliver*, thus allowing each member of the team to focus on his or her own deliverables

Achieve these three pillars and your team will function as a highly effective group.

25. At the end of each day, ask yourself, "What did I accomplish today that moved the project forward?" If you can't think of anything, you are doing something wrong.

26. No matter where you find yourself in the life cycle of your project, it is never too late to assess your goals, methodology, and purpose. It is critically important to the morale of your team to ensure the assumptions, values, and beliefs about what the team is supposed to do are explicitly laid out and communicated to necessary parties. The team must have clear, common, and integrated goals to support the shared vision of what things should look like when the project ends.

27. Don't lie, misrepresent your achievements, or attempt to claim credit that does not belong to you. It's only a matter of time before it catches up to you, and when it does, your integrity will suffer. Effective leaders know how to give credit when it is due and how to reward those who properly deserve it. Recognize your primary mission as a leader and maintain your priorities as such.

28. Your reputation, and therefore your effectiveness, will suffer if you consistently fail to return phone calls or e-mail.

29. If asked to manage a project that requires skills outside your expertise or components you are truly unfamiliar with, seek the assistance of others who are experienced in the subject and whom you trust. If you can't assign them directly to the project team, determine if you can secure commitments from them as subject matter experts for a small amount of time on a regular basis, such as five hours a

week or one hour a day. This arrangement can help you and your assigned experts demonstrate a level of effectiveness that is possible without compromising other organizational goals, and without needing to ask senior management to negotiate reporting lines.

If you are unable to secure subject matter experts to help you, remain very mindful of your limited abilities. Don't get taken in by flattery or persuasion. Make it clear to those requesting your services that you are not the right person for the job. It is better to do this early and avoid the criticism later.

30. Document everything. This doesn't mean you need to publish everything, but maintaining notes on as much of the project as you can will enable you to elevate your position as the subject matter expert and therefore become an invaluable member of the team. This means carrying a notebook and pen with you no matter where you go throughout the day. Many smartphones have voice recorders, which provide a quick and convenient way to document pieces of information. As you make notes and talk to different people, it will become easier to connect the dots and maintain your knowledge base.

Case Study: Document Everything

At the height of an intense project, one that had significant financial consequences if not completed on time, Carla, the project manager, met with Timothy, the executive sponsor of an application development group, to outline several options toward completing the project's objective. These options included a balance of the triple constraint: time, cost, and quality.

After a long discussion, Timothy told Carla, "Make quality the highest priority of the options. My team always produces the highest quality work, and we're not about to stop now."

Carla pointed out that maintaining high quality would increase the cost and likely extend the time line of the project.

"What you don't appreciate, Carla," said Timothy in a stern voice, "is the *real* cost of putting lower quality code into the environment. It will cost a lot more—and take much more time—if we don't do it right the first time!"

Understanding the direction clearly, Carla immediately communicated this approach to senior stakeholders and her management. Everyone took action based on the direction Timothy articulated.

A week later, when the details were raised concerning just how much cost was involved and the extent of the schedule extension, Timothy denied ever having the conversation with Carla. He "didn't recall" any options she presented to deliver the project on time.

Carla's integrity was called into question. She felt deeply embarrassed before her project team, stakeholders, and management.

Analysis:

Carla had the experience and fortitude to meet with a senior member of the organization and outline the options, allowing this senior individual to make an informed decision. After the meeting, Carla neglected to send a note requesting written confirmation, perhaps due to fear of appearing not to trust the senior manager, or of suggesting that his word was not good enough.

Lesson:

Carla learned that asking someone to confirm a decision in writing does not suggest mistrust, but rather demonstrates the acumen to substantiate a spoken agreement. Had she written out the options, which may have permitted Timothy an opportunity to correct his position without the need to lie about the original conversation, she could have saved face.

Always follow up with a written acknowledgment of an important decision reached through conversation. It may be best not to copy a lot of people when you seek this acknowledgment. In this case, if Carla had sent a note to Timothy verifying his decision, and he had responded with acknowledgment, she could then have forwarded the acknowledgment to the appropriate people. Alternatively, had she sent a note only to Timothy and he had changed his mind, he would have appreciated Carla's tact in making it easy for him to reverse course without the scrutiny of a broad audience.

---

31. When you are the project manager and responsible for delivering to a customer, the customer will view you as

the face of all the teams and work streams involved in delivering the project. This is not only wholly appropriate, but necessary. Avoid distinguishing yourself from the work streams, such as saying, "The development group is responsible for that; I'm the project manager."

32. Do not be fooled by resources who shower you with compliments in an attempt to befriend you under false pretenses. Your duty is to complete the project on time. Performing favors for someone else will ultimately undermine your effectiveness.

Case Study: The Phony Friend

In a classic case of pretense, a technical project resource, Richard, befriended a newly assigned project manager, Scott. Richard made certain to highlight himself as a person "in the know" about everyone on the project and how things worked in the organization. Richard offered help to Scott and even offered to fill him in over drinks and dinners.

From Scott's perspective, a friendship was blooming, and he had an inside track on some of the project participants. After a few weeks, however, Scott realized that his new "friend" was a bit lazy and often needed extra time to complete tasks. Continuing his disappointing participation, Richard wanted to trade drinks for a blind eye toward his inabilities.

Scott found himself in a very awkward position and knew he had to change the dynamic. He couldn't allow Richard to get away with late or missed deliverables without other team members noticing. He also knew that having accepted drinks and dinners from Richard in the past would make it awkward to discipline Richard as he would any other team member.

As Scott contemplated how to address the situation with Richard, he found himself wishing he had never accepted this "friendship." Deciding that the best way to correct a mistake was to admit to it and start down the right path as soon as possible, Scott arranged a lunch with Richard. This time, Scott paid for their lunch.

At lunch, Scott took a deep breath and said, "This is awkward. I value your friendship, and I like to socialize with you after work. But it cannot interfere with our responsibilities at the office. I take this assignment very seriously and want to do the best job I can. For that, I need everyone's commitment to do the same, including yours."

"Oh sure, sure," Richard said with an ingratiating smile.

"You've had some late deliverables and implied requests for special treatment. As much as I may like you as a friend, I cannot allow anyone on the team to receive special treatment. Do you understand?"

Richard nodded, looking solemn.

"Is there anything outside work interfering with your ability to do a good job?"

"No," Richard replied.

"I need the participation of everyone on the team to the best of his or her ability. Otherwise, the whole team will suffer. As project manager, I need to protect the team. Understood?"

Richard got the message. He didn't like it, but he did gain respect for Scott that day. Scott felt unburdened of the awkwardness of dealing with a friend who wanted special treatment. Scott also learned never to depend on the admiration of others.

---

33. Time management is a vital skill for any successful project manager. If you have not yet mastered a time management methodology that works for you, seek a course, a book, or an application that will suggest a variety of methods and determine which one is appropriate for you. Without command of time management skills, you will not succeed as a project manager or leader.

34. When developing a project schedule, make certain to use and repeat the word "date" in your correspondence with project resources. Although obvious, perhaps, this will reinforce your need for dates (estimated or actual) that will keep your schedules accurate and meaningful. If a project resource gives a useless, yet typical response such as "sometime next week" or "I'm not sure," or if they can't determine an appropriate duration at all, ask for best-case, worst-case, and most likely scenarios. Then take the mean (average) of the three as your planning duration.

35. Regardless of where you work or the culture, managing an important project requires eight to ten hours a day. Anything less means you are not doing everything you can,

or the project is quite small and you have the ability to take on more work. Devoting eight to ten hours to managing your projects is especially necessary if you are managing more than one project. Benjamin Franklin said, "If you want something done, give it to a busy person."

36. Evaluate your resources on their deeds rather than their words. Everyone is different, with diverse backgrounds and personalities, which may influence how they go about getting things done. While it is important for team members to comply with the governance model, their methods may seem foreign at times. Remedy any questions by holding team members accountable for their deliverables. In the simplest terms, if a team member gets his or her job done in an effective manner, the delivery may outweigh the method. Conversely, if a team member fails to consistently deliver, but offers many words of explanation, accountability is lost. In the realm of project management, we are all judged by what we deliver and not what we start.

37. Project resources come and go. It is quite rare to maintain a consistent project team throughout the entire life cycle of a major project. As such, prepare your "handover" or "knowledge transfer" templates and procedures well before someone leaves your project team or the announcement of a transition is made. This will help ensure minimal impact to your project and prevent unnecessary confusion within your team.

38. Don't assume that your project resources will take it upon themselves to execute a solution, even one that is well discussed and vetted. As project manager, it is your role to approve the direction and take responsibility for its execution. Resources will perform better if they a have an e-mail directing them to carry out a task or implement a

solution, providing them with the justification they desire. This is especially true in situations that are tense or have high visibility.

39. Accountability must go both ways. When updating your stakeholders, especially during a one-on-one situation, follow up the communication with an e-mail that reiterates the salient points of the discussion. Discussion, agreement, and support are fleeting without the backup of written acknowledgment. It is very easy for a stakeholder to reverse position or deny a discussion ever took place when there is nothing to reference it. This could leave you in a very difficult position later on. Holding senior management accountable in an appropriate fashion is the mark of a seasoned project manager.

40. Take every opportunity to informally socialize with or meet senior management so that they become more familiar and comfortable with you, thereby permitting a free exchange of ideas and feedback. Senior management should understand that you remain accountable to them for the outcome of the project, and that you will not abandon the post no matter how rough the seas get. They need to know you are not an "order taker" and indeed make mistakes, but that you also take ownership of mistakes, correct them, and remain a source of broad information that no one else commands.

41. The actions of a project manager should be almost unnoticeable. When a project is moving along smoothly, people are sometimes tempted to question the need for a project manager. However, when you take the skilled project manager out of the equation, a project is much more likely to miss deadlines and exceed budgets. Don't grow concerned if your hard work seems to go unnoticed

and others receive more credit. If the project is executed professionally and delivered on time and within budget, you'll soon have the credit you deserve.

42. It is very important, especially in large organizations, to ensure that everyone on the project team has an assigned role and responsibility. This role may be different from or contrary to a resource's corporate title. Everyone on the project team must know the value each team member will add and how the overall responsibility and dependency for the project's outcome is shared. The allocation of resources is often a confusing aspect of project teams, especially in teams that have members spread across the globe or mixed across different disciplines. Further confusion is brought about when corporate titles delay project team members from seeking updates or action. ("She's a managing director; I'm a vice president. I can't ask her for an update!") Your team will function better if they understand and contribute to how resources function.

43. From time to time, assess the performance rating of your team. Do you manage an effective team that can respond to necessary change quickly? Is your team working in a coordinated fashion? Are their deliverables consistently impressive? If the answer is no to any question, then your team is not operating effectively. This can only endure for so long before project deliverables are missed and morale deteriorates. Make certain you have a plan to keep your team operating at a high performance level. There are scores of books that offer theories on creating effective teams, underscoring the magnitude of this problem. It impacts many, many organizations. Investing time in discovering how to create an effective team may prove to be your success X factor. A great resource is *The Wisdom of Teams*, by Jon R. Katzenbach and Douglas K. Smith.

44. Don't forget to regularly renew your team's spirit, especially during the project life cycle. Most project managers think celebrations should be reserved for project completion. Keeping your team refreshed and renewed is best achieved through regular, repeated recognition of milestones and major accomplishments. Make a big deal of your team's achievements and reward them. In some cases, you may need to spend a little of your own money, but consider this a cost of doing business. A very small reward goes a very long way with team members. Something as simple as a team gathering, where a few words are said about the success, can inspire other team members to reach higher and perform better. Everyone loves a shout-out. "An enterprise can never be planned and carried on without abilities of skilled people. And those people must have principle or they cannot have confidence enough in each other."—John Adams

Case Study: Managing in the Aftermath of the September 11, 2001, Terrorist Attacks

It's difficult to comprehend now, in 2014, but the world of corporate technology infrastructure before the September 11, 2001, terrorist attacks was quite different. This is perhaps best illustrated by one global bank, with offices around the world, that maintained its New York City production data center and disaster recovery data center in the same city, in the same building, separated by only a few floors. September 11, 2001, changed the mind-set of corporate leaders around the globe forever.

What followed those attacks was a broad-based effort to strategically locate data centers in cities less prone to attack. Companies also separated production and disaster recovery infrastructure by very significant distances, further ensuring that a disaster would not cripple their technology services.

In 2002 this global bank began a migration of their corporate technology infrastructure to new, nondescript, ultrasecure locations in remote parts of the United States. It was a major initiative and the board of directors' main priority for the long-term health of the firm. Several programs were set up to coordinate the migration of platforms, servers, networks, storage, and more to the new sites, all while maintaining business operations that relied on this infrastructure.

The migration premise, approved by the most senior leaders of the firm, called for a "lift and shift" approach, meaning the infrastructure was powered down late on a Friday night, then placed on a truck and driven to the new location by Saturday afternoon. The technical team set up and configured the infrastructure for restored operation by Sunday afternoon. This approach minimized cost by using existing hardware for the majority of moves, minimized risk by moving a small subset of hardware each week, and allowed reasonable back-out capability if something went terribly wrong. The program parameters called for full business operation to be restored by three o'clock each Sunday afternoon.

The program was quite big, with many interconnected parties that were all dependent on the success of one another. The team setting up the servers could not do much if the storage and network teams didn't provide the necessary connectivity. As with most highly visible and important initiatives, the bank hired a third party, in this case IBM, to assist with the program and be accountable for the delivery of the intended solution.

With thousands of stakeholders, hundreds of project participants, scores of project managers, and a tremendous amount of pressure to ensure that business operations did not suffer, a broad global team came together to execute the plan.

Many people did tremendously good work under some of the toughest conditions. They ultimately succeeded in relocating the entire complement of infrastructure from New York City to new locations, all without adversely impacting business operations. It took almost three years to complete the initiative. There were countless lessons learned that helped guide future projects to more successful delivery. One such lesson highlighted the importance of accountability.

Of the many projects managers assigned to the migration initiative, two project managers were charged with managing the relocation of distributed UNIX and WinTel infrastructure. Recognizing the mutual dependencies their projects faced, they collaborated very closely. Their abilities to manage risk, coordinate resources, and ensure consistent reporting was much more effective when they coordinated their efforts, and they maximized the opportunity to do so.

As the weekend migrations commenced, the project managers orchestrated an environment that provided the best opportunity for the vast technical teams to succeed. They remained at the New York City data center late into Friday night until the allocated infrastructure had been loaded onto the trucks. They often performed administrative tasks such as putting stickers on the servers to make certain the right equipment was targeted for relocation.

Once the trucks were loaded, the project managers drove overnight to the new location and met the trucks as they arrived on Saturday. They provided schedules to the technical teams so everyone knew who had to show up and when. After a few hours of sleep in a nearby hotel, the project managers visited local bakeries and provided coffee and breakfast to the teams as they arrived for their early morning shifts. The project managers arranged mandatory breaks for those who worked overnight. They set up a system of technical health checks that allowed continuous confidence in the progress of restored capability.

The concept of a blog had not been widely adopted in 2002, so the project managers maintained a running list of lessons learned to share with key stakeholders as the migrations continued. The project managers returned to New York City for Monday morning and walked the floors with the affected users to ensure the effects of the move were made clear. Issues were reported back to the technical teams in the remote data center, resolved, and then logged for submission to the knowledge base. It was an incredibly challenging routine, both physically and mentally.

Overall, each weekend's migration stage (effectively a project in itself) was a qualified success, and the issues decreased with each passing weekend. The project managers looked after every detail and never abandoned the mind-set that they remained accountable for everything that happened during their watch. No job was too big or too small for them to take on. Not surprisingly, the members of the broad teams, including IBM, began to rely on this mind-set of end-to-end accountability.

After a few months, the entire routine was scripted, and the project managers orchestrated each operation with impressive precision. As migrations continued, stakeholders developed increasing confidence in the project, especially the technical resources. What emerged was an overall winning team that shared in the success of each weekend's operation.

At about this time, the two project managers were called into the office of one of the senior sponsors and asked, "Why are you spending so much money each weekend? Your expenses are piling up: hotel, gas, food. It's too much. The teams should know what to do by now. There's no reason for you to go each weekend simply to direct traffic."

Despite detailed explanations, the project managers were unsuccessful in their bid to convince the sponsor that the cost of their coordination efforts—and the presence of a single point of accountability for everyone on the team—played a critical role in each weekend's success. They were told, unequivocally, not to work the next weekend.

On that Friday night, the project managers followed their instructions and attempted to coordinate the teams via phone and e-mail.

Without their presence, which included looking after the technical teams to ensure they had food and requisite sleep, coordinating the truck arrival and departure, notifying team members when to show up based on the traffic and weather conditions on the ground, and ensuring that breakfast welcomed everyone when they arrived, much of the management direction was lost. Infrastructure that should have been part of the move didn't make it onto the truck; other teams arrived at the new data center much earlier than needed, then fell asleep waiting for the trucks to arrive; and mass confusion mounted when it was discovered there was no one person in charge.

Monday morning proved particularly difficult for the technical teams. The end-user complaints grew as the business day progressed. Access to specific migration information was missing, critical files were not available, and tempers rose as frustration filled the offices of senior management.

Senior stakeholders called the project managers in, demanding an explanation. "Why, after so many months of uneventful migrations did we find ourselves in the middle of a disaster with financial and reputational impact?"

The brief but sobering explanation didn't take long to resonate. By adopting the mind-set of 100 percent accountability, the project managers had ensured that every aspect of each migration weekend was sorted out and organized for success. This accountability permitted them the authority to direct the team members (often of senior rank) and the confidence to understand precisely what was needed and when. They had successfully eliminated the question of "Whose job is it?" by treating any job without an owner as their own. Absent the project managers, accountability was lost, and execution suffered.

The issue of cost never came up again. The project managers participated in every migration weekend through the conclusion of the project.

Analysis:

Management grew complacent upon seeing successful results week after week, and shifted their concern from execution risk to increasing cost, never connecting the dots between the two. They mistakenly believed the project teams could operate on some form of collective memory, despite the constantly shifting personnel taking part in each weekend.

Lesson:

As a project manager, don't be surprised if your good work leads others to doubt your value. Do the right thing and maintain your loyalty to the mission you have been entrusted to deliver. The confidence you draw from knowing what is right will help you face those who doubt you. Absorb criticism without misinterpreting it as a personal attack.

Chapter Three
Communication

*The single biggest problem in communication is
the illusion that it has taken place.*
—George Bernard Shaw

Communication is the most important aspect of any
project. It is the most useful tool in the project manager's
tool chest. There is no limit to the opportunity to improve
communication skills, which include verbal, written, and
even body language. If you focus on nothing else, ensure
that you can communicate effectively in all manner of
situations. Communication most often takes place in
presentations, written documents, and group discussions.
It is not confined to dialogue.

Meetings

45. Consider it a general rule that you should spend twice the
     time preparing for a meeting as the meeting is scheduled
     to last. The more you prepare for a meeting, the more
     value you can offer the attendees. Nothing demonstrates
     a project manager's qualifications better than a well-run
     meeting with clear objectives that are accomplished in the
     time frame scheduled. Many will see this as a microcosm
     of your effectiveness and abilities.

46. Communicate your meeting details, such as the date, time
     (including time zone when applicable), building, conference
     room, audio bridge, and any supporting documentation, in
     as many forms as possible. There is increased chance of
     participation if you can limit the possibility of resources
     forgetting, overlooking, or needing to hunt for meeting
     information just as the meeting starts.

47. When scheduling a meeting, whether as a single occurrence
     or one that repeats on a regular basis, take the time to
     research your key participants' calendars and determine
     the most favorable time to meet. If you cannot identify
     a time slot when all key members are free, contact them
     individually with three suggested time slots and explain
     the importance of the meeting and what its goal is. Allow
     them to send delegates of their choosing, but remain clear
     that accountability rests with them. Failing to do this leg
     work ahead of time puts at risk not only the ability of key
     participants to attend, but also your reputation as someone
     who is organized, thoughtful, and creative.

48. When scheduling a thirty-minute meeting, try to schedule
     the start at the top of the hour instead of half past the hour.
     This will reduce the likelihood that attendees will try to

double book themselves and arrive late—or not at all—to your meeting.

49. Meetings must start and end on time. It is the project manager's responsibility to control the meeting. If you schedule a meeting at ten o'clock, start the roll call at 10:03. You may extend a short courtesy period to your attendees, but guard against extending it for more than a few minutes.

50. Always publish an agenda for each meeting you chair. An agenda communicates your goals for meeting success and allows others to adequately prepare. Publish your agenda at least one business day prior to the meeting. At the meeting, distribute printed copies of the agenda. Remember, if you don't publish an agenda, others will bring their own—and they won't let you know what it is until the meeting starts, which will likely lead to a chaotic discussion. Invest the time to create an appropriate and meaningful agenda that will push the project forward. A good agenda leads to an effective meeting and will therefore add value for each participant. If you have been invited to a meeting with no published agenda, ask for one. If you are not provided with one, write up a list of topics you want to cover and e-mail the list to the chairperson.

51. A well-run meeting is invaluable. People often object to meetings or attend without alacrity because they believe most meetings are run poorly and achieve little, if anything. A well-run meeting that settles an objective (no matter how small), produces action items, records the testimony of what was said, and adheres to the published agenda is quite instrumental. At the end of a meeting, if you have covered all of your agenda items yet believe the meeting was unsuccessful, change the agenda for future meetings but not the approach.

52. Communicate issues and risks in status reports and highlight them at the beginning of a meeting to ensure that everyone is informed. Read the open issues and risks aloud, especially when senior managers attend. However, avoid allowing the team to divert the agenda in favor of trying to solve the issue or risk, if such diversion compromises the meeting purpose. A well-managed project will allocate appropriate time for teams to brainstorm in an alternate venue and then report their conclusions at a subsequent status meeting.

53. A meeting is a great way to obtain project status, but it is no substitute for one-on-one conversations with individual team members. If you can arrange one-on-one discussions with all team members within a month, you will gain their trust and a better understanding of the project's potential hot spots.

54. Always state clearly a meeting's purpose, both in writing (within the agenda) and verbally at the start of the meeting. Never assume that meeting attendees are aware of the objective. Make it prominent in your agenda. Likewise, clearly state when the meeting is over. Use the phrase such as "We are adjourned," or "Thank you for attending; this meeting is concluded." This will enable those on a conference bridge to clearly determine when they can hang up.

55. Discourage team members from continuing an important discussion and reaching conclusions after the meeting has concluded. Team members will often gather after a meeting, perhaps in the hall or on their way back to their desks, and will privately settle or reach agreement on an important issue. While this may seem like progress, and perhaps it is, there is risk of alienating team members who

are not part of the "private conversation." When important decisions are made outside of collaborative venues, morale suffers and effectiveness can dip. If you become aware that a private meeting has reached a conclusion or resolved an issue, make certain to highlight the results in your minutes or at the next meeting, without embarrassing anyone or publicly faulting team members.

56. When inviting members to a meeting, be careful to not overinvite. Conventional wisdom suggests a correlation between the number of people attending a meeting and the ability to accomplish objectives. Omit those individuals who only need to know the meeting results as opposed to the details of how those results were achieved. If necessary or significantly helpful, personally review the meeting minutes with those interested in the results.

Case Study: Add Up All the Salaries

During the middle of the financial crisis in 2008, a broadly attended meeting that included many senior individuals was interrupted by one of the most senior leaders of the firm in a loud and frustrated voice. He demanded to know how much this unproductive, mismanaged meeting was costing the company. He said, "I bet if I add up everyone's salary here and calculate the hourly rate, multiplying that by the two and a half hours we sat here with nothing accomplished, we would learn that this meeting is costing our shareholders more than a million dollars. Who called this meeting? I want his head!" The project manager wanted to crawl under a rock.

Analysis:

An unproductive meeting can do a lot more harm than simply failing to accomplish a goal or resolve an issue. Sooner or later, someone will recognize the lack of effectiveness in the gathering. That someone might be a low-ranking member of the team or a senior stakeholder. Either way, real damage can occur if an ineffective meeting is allowed to continue.

Lesson:

Prepare for your meetings to ensure that you know exactly what the meeting is intended to accomplish and whose attendance is required to reach that accomplishment. If a meeting is not moving in the right direction and is essentially a waste of time, then you, the project manager, should call for adjournment and regroup with a better strategy.

57.   Actively attempt to reduce miscellaneous and ineffective meetings. Respect the time of the resources on your invite list and recognize that many are likely committed to more than one project or initiative. If a scheduling conflict arises for resources, take action to resolve the conflict and don't leave the decision exclusively to the resource. This means you must secure commitment to your meeting well before the meeting takes place.

58.   Just as you take pains to eliminate unnecessary meetings for your project team, scrutinize the meetings you are invited to. Don't blindly accept every meeting invitation; examine which meetings you can add value to and which you can't,

and then accept or decline appropriately. Likewise, examine which meetings add value to your efforts and which don't. As a project manager, you have far too many valuable exercises you must accomplish to keep your project under control. They won't get completed if you are in endless and unnecessary meetings all week.

59. Discourage team members from bringing laptops or tablets to a meeting. There is a good chance they will use your meeting to work on something other than your project. At the very best, they will be distracted and tempted to remain so throughout the meeting. Some may argue that a tablet is helpful to display the agenda or meeting material. Avoid the need for tablets by printing the agenda and meeting material so you can ensure greater attention among your participants. If a participant has electronic material germane to the meeting, arrange a projector so everyone can benefit from seeing it.

60. Whenever possible, avoid attending or allowing others to attend meetings over the phone. Communication is enhanced when people can see your expressions and body language. With today's technology, video meetings are more accessible and permit greater collaboration among teams. Meeting in person also helps ensure the attention of your audience. It sometimes requires extra effort, such as visiting another floor or going outside in poor weather, but the determination put into meeting others in person will go a long way toward building relationships before you actually need them.

61. When you must hold a meeting over the phone, carefully prepare the space you will conduct the meeting from. If it's your office or cube, turn off your monitor and silence your mobile phone. Remove distracting elements that may

capture your attention. Ensure that you have a quiet clock or watch available to keep track of time. Have your agenda and supporting documentation printed and laid out in front of you. Do not attempt to multitask; although no one can see you, people can tell when you are attempting to do many things at once. Remain courteous to your meeting participants by speaking slowly with enunciation. Don't chew gum, mumble, tap your pen, or create background noise that can distract attention from the meeting purpose.

62. Avoid attending or chairing a meeting while on your cell phone, especially if you are driving a car or riding public transportation. It is simply bad form. Despite pleas for forgiveness, participants will draw the conclusion that you did not prepare or are incapable of time management.

63. If permitted, record all meetings. This allows you to focus on making points and exercising control without worrying about taking notes. It's also a great way to keep people honest. Store all recordings in a secure place, accessible to only yourself, and resist any requests to share the recordings. During a project, or even after it is completed, you never know when you will need to recheck your minutes. If ever challenged on what you documented, the recording can help you determine the appropriate way to handle the situation.

64. It is perfectly acceptable to hold a meeting by yourself. If no one shows up to your scheduled meeting and you find yourself the lone attendee, hold the meeting and note the attendance in the minutes, which should consist of one sentence under the heading of *Discussion Points*: "As there was no representation from any of the assigned work streams, the meeting adjourned without any action or purpose." Publish the meeting minutes as usual. The

five-minute investment may come in handy when someone later inquires about project progress—or the lack of it.

65. Resist the temptation to skip publishing the meeting minutes or to cancel a meeting because you are unprepared. Often the easy way to handle a situation is not the correct way to handle it. If you find yourself unprepared for a standing meeting, use the time to review the project fundamentals (risks, issues, dependencies, and constraints) and see if anyone holds a contrary view. If the meeting was intended to accomplish a specific mission, yet you are unprepared to achieve that mission, then you must postpone the meeting. Frequent postponements, however, will sacrifice your reputation as someone in charge.

Written Communications

66. Review human resource policies and procedures when you first arrive at a company. Many companies have strict rules regarding e-mail, instant messaging, and Web usage that may affect your planned methodology for project management. The last thing a project manager needs on his or her record is a violation of any kind.

67. Take time to write your correspondence carefully and with adequate thought. Strive for communication so clear that honest people can't misunderstand it and dishonest people can't misrepresent it. Reread everything you write to ensure that your point or question is conveyed accurately and with the appropriate tone. If you are assigning a task or requesting assistance, attempt to convey the following in one paragraph:

   a.   Your question or point

b.   The date you need a response

c.   A suggested answer (if asking a question)

This will better enable your reader(s) to identify what you expect from them and when. Be succinct in your e-mail correspondence. Avoid at all costs a long e-mail. They often confuse readers, and most will only recall those sentences that they agree with. And for Pete's sake, don't use "emoticons" or shorthand slang such as *LOL*, *ROFL*, or *THX 4 UR Hlp* in your correspondence. Save this for the kids.

68.   In this digital age, everyone is surrounded by data and often subjected to data overload. Before making your manager aware of something, even in the framework of a status update, analyze the information. Present it with the necessary interpretation and business intelligence to clarify what she or he needs to know or do next. When preparing messages to stakeholders, sponsors, or senior management, make them brief and clear. Articulate the current perceptions of the parties, the risks and opportunities, and the possible solutions. Share your insight, and encourage your team members to do so. Don't forget: a picture is worth a thousand words. Visual representations help a lot if accompanied with intelligence.

69.   If you receive an e-mail communication and are uncertain of its purpose or of what action to take, ask! Don't assume, even if you are on the copy (cc) list, that someone included you on an e-mail distribution for no reason or that no response on your part is required. If you don't follow up, you may leave the sender believing that silence is acceptance or that you clearly understand what is required or requested of you.

49

70. When using e-mail, especially in an effort to escalate or criticize, avoid the temptation to copy (cc) everyone. While you may get some type of response from this tactic, chances are greater the approach will hurt you down the road. Don't underestimate the power of simple courtesy.

71. Attempt to avoid using e-mail as your documentation repository. E-mail is often lost or deleted and some companies assign limitations to mailbox size. If you make the mistake of relying on e-mail for historical record, you may find yourself out of luck.

72. Avoid complex, ostentatious e-mail signatures. Your e-mail signature should include basic information such as your name, title, and at least one—preferably two—forms of voice contact. The best signatures are conservative and do not detract from the body of the e-mail. A signature is simply a means for others to review additional information about you. Pictures, quotations, and fancy script are not necessary or productive. Configure your mail program to include your signature on replies as well as the messages you originate. It is important that everyone connected to your project or program have a convenient way to contact you.

73. Strive to keep your distribution list to the minimum required. Copying unnecessary people on an e-mail, even one of congratulations, risks a negative reaction; they may read your first and even second message, but if neither provides information that directly affects them, you can be sure they will not read your third message. Choose your audience carefully, asking yourself, "Why would he or she care?"

74. Be mindful of whom you copy on your e-mail correspondence, especially when you do so under the

guise of keeping others informed. Most senior leaders do not have the opportunity to read and absorb every e-mail they receive, especially when the correspondence goes back and forth several times between parties. Do not forward correspondence with the term *FYI*; asking someone to read an entire e-mail chain and perform his or her own interpretation is a junior mistake. If you must forward a piece of information to someone, especially someone senior, take an extra few minutes to include a brief interpretation stating why you believe it important that the recipient understand this information.

75. Never assume people read their e-mail or listen to voice mail. Make it part of your routine to follow up, perhaps informally, to verify that critical messages have been received and understood. Sending an e-mail does not constitute communication. As tempting as it is to blame someone for failing to listen to a voice mail or read an e-mail in a timely manner, the fact remains that the project manager is responsible for controlling communication and ensuring that critical messages are received and understood.

76. Don't immediately assume that someone is ignoring you when you haven't heard from him or her in a while, despite numerous e-mail, voice mail, and personal attempts to track him or her down. There is sometimes temptation to lash out, copy the world, and escalate the delinquency. While firing a rocket may be tempting, it's better to take the high road and reflect support and concern, rather than representing yourself as an oppressor, especially if the missing person has something you need. Exhaust all the possibilities and avoid (as much as possible) e-mail or documented requests that may come to appear over the top once you have an explanation. Calling, stopping by, or

reaching out through a friend, colleague, or supervisor is much more effective.

77. Remove any emotional language from your meeting minutes. If an argument occurs during a meeting, do not rehash it in the minutes. Rather, use the phrase "after a brief discussion." By revisiting an argument on paper, you become an adversary to the speakers, and team members will avoid future meetings.

78. Be factual in your communication. Opinion is sometimes valuable, but when you mingle facts and opinion, the audience is left to separate the two, and they likely won't do so accurately. Review your statements carefully and remove anything inappropriate or emotionally charged. It is simply good practice not to let emotions enter your message. Don't publish anything you wouldn't want to see on the front page of the *New York Times*.

79. When reporting your project status, assume that it will ultimately reach a very wide audience, even if your project is not high profile. Utilizing a variety of written reports to communicate your project's status will help you broadcast your message in consistent and meaningful formats.

80. When communicating in writing, take pains to make your statements effective, highlighting not only what you did, but why it is important to the reader. Structure your statements in business language and avoid technical jargon. Always start with the business benefit, then highlight the achievement, and finally include any additional clarity that will assist the reader with understanding the merit of the action, issue, or proposal discussed.

81. When authoring meeting minutes, start with a copy of the agenda. This will enable you to correctly capture the invitees, discussion topics, action items, and so on. It will also enable you to remain consistent in general format between agenda and minutes. The time you spend authoring meeting minutes is a valuable opportunity to perform follow-ups and gain further control of your project. As you transcribe your notes and/or recording into prose, spend time updating project schedules, sending e-mails, making phone calls, and generally following through on needs and promises flagged during the meeting.

82. Avoid publishing the minutes of a meeting you did not chair. Publishing good minutes takes time and effort. If you do not run a meeting, you have no control over how long it runs or what is discussed. In the same manner, don't ask someone else to produce minutes of a meeting you chair. As a project manager, you must control the message.

83. To be effective, minutes should be published no more than twenty-four hours after the meeting.

84. Make it a practice to avoid publishing documents, authoring e-mail, or making decisions in a rushed manner, especially if you are attempting to demonstrate progress. Haste certainly makes waste, but also risks a mistake that you can't easily correct, especially if you publish to a wide audience. Allocate enough time to permit careful review of all your work.

85. Status reports are only useful if they communicate needs and/or new information. Reports for the sake of reporting are a waste of time.

86. If there's one thing that frustrates project teams more than a poorly run project, it's the necessity to provide the same information over and over in different formats. It's the responsibility of the project manager to determine how to limit the overhead of the project team and enable them to focus on their work, rather than the duty of providing updates in various forms to various groups on various schedules. Make it a priority to determine which updates are needed by whom and when, in order to ensure a minimalist approach to soliciting information from your teams. A regular audit of reporting activity is a good idea to keep reporting under control. A challenge to the status quo may prove necessary, but this is part of the project manager's job description.

87. Publish all your documents in locked PDF format. This prevents others from changing what you publish and seals the record for historical purposes. It also makes your documents visible across different devices, such as smartphones and tablets.

88. Avoid naming a document with the words *final* or *master* in the name, such as *Project XYZ Status Report FINAL*. While it's understandable that you may keep multiple versions of a document, when you distribute it, remove the word *final* and replace it with a date and time. In the event you need to update the document, you will look foolish either distributing another document with *final* in its title or naming something *final final*.

89. Always proofread your work. There is no excuse for careless mistakes. People will judge you on your ability to command your language. Proofread all documentation, including agendas, minutes, and plans. Take the time to reread the documents you author. Correcting spelling,

grammar and, more importantly, facts is imperative. The time it takes to correct a document prior to publication is nothing compared to the time it will take you to correct the impact of a careless mistake afterward.

90. Most of the productivity tools available to project managers are not commonly installed on the broader population's desktops, such as Microsoft Visio or Microsoft Project. If you use these tools as a communication vehicle for your projects, make certain to print documentation from them in PDF format before you distribute them. This will make your work accessible to a wider audience and improve the chances of receiving valuable feedback. The easier it is for people to access and review your documents, the more often they will do so. Before sending, ask yourself, "What will the recipient do with this?" or "What do I want the recipient to do with this?"

91. Invest time to develop a set of standard templates for meeting agendas, minutes, status reports, presentations, and other written communications that you and others can utilize as models. This will enable you to accomplish two objectives: (1) avoid confusion caused by the use of many different formats, and (2) create an ability to further market yourself. If the templates you create add value and permit the easy relay of information, others will use them.

92. If possible, post your status reports, meeting minutes, metrics, accomplishments, issues, and risks on a website, Microsoft SharePoint site, or wiki page for anyone to access and comment on. Recognize that in the twenty-first century, most people are mobile a good portion of the time and therefore appreciate status reports that are easy to read and interpret from their mobile devices. When stakeholders understand your efforts, they will appreciate

the accountability you take for your projects. Trust in your accountability is priceless, and just like the value of your good word, it's earned.

Case Study: Changing With The Times—The Dashboard

Upon the advent of widespread smartphone usage, many successful project managers had difficulty adapting to the new ways of doing business. In one such case, an experienced and respected project manager, Miriam, who was set in her ways, maintained a very comprehensive project dashboard, developed in Microsoft PowerPoint. Every Friday, she e-mailed it to her stakeholders and management. In years past, she had received accolades for the report.

However, as more and more people moved to smartphones, they received the dashboard on their mobile device as an attachment, one that was not yet viewable on most phones. People received the e-mail, tried to view the dashboard, were unable to do so, and moved on.

Not recognizing the problem, Miriam continued her publication for months, until a significant issue arose that had potential to derail the project. Although the issue was well articulated and documented in her dashboard, and the dashboard was published like clockwork each Friday, a growing number of stakeholders were unaware of the issue. They relied on their mobile devices and were acclimated to the fact they could not view Miriam's attachments. The issue was therefore never acted upon by the right people.

Only when it was too late and the issue had been brought to light by other means did Miriam realize that no one was reading her dashboard. Her years of praise were suddenly called into question. She was held accountable for not communicating a major issue at an early enough stage. The lesson she learned is underscored by a quotation: "It is not the strongest of the species that survives, nor the most intelligent that survives. It is the one that is most adaptable to change. In the struggle for survival, the fittest win out at the expense of their rivals because they succeed in adapting themselves best to their environment."—Leon C. Megginson

---

93. We live in a time when people can and do work from everywhere and beyond standard working hours. Smartphones, tablets, and work-from-anywhere functionality allow people to conduct business outside the office or when others are asleep. As a project manager, you must ensure that any message you deliver electronically, especially if it's germane to your project, takes into consideration the fact that someone will review it outside the office, in a different time zone, and perhaps on a mobile device or public kiosk. Therefore, don't put your entire update in an attachment or expect that everyone has the ability to view the update from a fully functional desktop computer. Be courteous and include a few sentences in your e-mail that summarize the update. Include the best time and manner to contact you with questions. You don't want a recipient replying to all when asking a question or

requesting clarification, especially if it is after your working hours. Controlling the message and governing the exchange are key attributes of any seasoned project manager.

94. Scheduling tools, such as Microsoft Project, are wonderful for tracking tasks and understanding their relationships to dates and other tasks. But don't assume everyone on the team understands the proper way to read a Gantt or resource chart. If you want to communicate status from Microsoft Project, use one of the built-in reports or translate the appropriate amount of detail into a presentation.

In-Person Communications

95. One of the most effective forms of communication a project manager can employ is informal exchange. Years ago, when much more of the population smoked, business leaders would often gather outside for a cigarette and sort through problems as they smoked. Much was accomplished in these relaxed exchanges. Trust was built and respect was strengthened. There was a lot to say for a group of colleagues meeting outside, exchanging views, and reaching agreements. Some of the bonds created in these forums are still in place today and continue to be venues to get things done, sometimes across organizations. To build upon this theme today, eat lunch away from your desk as often as possible, and always try to eat with someone else. People are more relaxed during lunch and may be more blunt and open about issues. You might get information or a perspective that you normally would not get during a meeting. If you are so overloaded that you do not have time to take thirty minutes for lunch, that is a sign that you need better organization.

96. All effective leaders know how to express themselves. Some people are born with the gift of expression, but most of us have to learn it as a skill, like many other attributes of leadership. If you have difficulty expressing yourself in a poised, nonvulgar, and informative manner, take the necessary steps to learn. Self-expression includes verbal communication, written communication, and body language. Attempt to master them all so that you can consistently express yourself in an engaging and convincing manner.

97. Recognize and adapt to the different customs of users in different countries, such as work hours, holidays, formatting, and etiquette. Respecting these will allow you to go much further in your effort to create partnerships. The website http://www.culturecrossing.net is a wonderful resource to help you understand cross-cultural etiquette.

98. When seeking greater accountability from your project team, make sure you are clear in your request: what you want, when you want it, and how you want it. If you lack clear communication and leave accountability open to interpretation, you will receive a mixture of responses and likely be disappointed.

Case Study: The Mailroom

For ten years Joe worked as supervisor of the national mailing division of a large industrial supplier of tool parts. He was promoted several times and eventually became the vice president of the company. The new

supervisor of the national mailing division, Bill, now reports to Joe.

At the beginning of the month when the mailing of
new brochures is scheduled, Joe stops by the national
mailing division to see how things are going. He checks
the orders and then says to Bill, "I see you're doing the
Midwest mailing first. I always started with the West
Coast mailing."

Bill responds, "Yes, Joe."

The following month, Joe again returns and notices
that the first mailings are still going to the Midwest.
He says to Bill, "You know, when I had this job, I always
found that mailing materials to the West Coast first
made the whole job simpler."

Bill responds, "That's one way of doing it, I guess."

The following month, Joe visits the department with
a real grimace on his face. He says to Bill, "You're still
doing the Midwest mailings first, I see."

Bill says, "Yes, sir."

Joe gives Bill a look of disdain and leaves in a huff. Bill
stands there not knowing why his boss is unhappy
with him.

Analysis:

Bill wants the West Coast mailing to go first. He thinks
that he's told Bill that and is unhappy that his orders
have been ignored. The fact is he thinks he told Bill

what to do, but he never really did. What he thought was an order, Bill perceived as an observation or suggestion.

Lesson:

Be as clear and direct as you can when giving direction to your team. Do not think that others will pick up on hints or casual comments.

---

99. Work with both senior and junior team members, but utilize different communication methods. Avoid communicating exclusively with senior members of the team. Learn to manage down and sideways as well as up. The ability to manage well in all directions could prove to be the hinge your success swings upon.

100. When asked to present the status of your project to a senior executive, such as the CEO, CTO, CFO, or CIO, who is not included in your normal status distributions and is perhaps unfamiliar with your specific project, focus on the overall methodology and story of the project. Provide, in succinct fashion, an executive summary that includes the following information:

  a. Situation (why the project exists, including the benefit and what goes away)

  b. Action (the methodology of the project and major work streams)

  c. Current state of the project's health

    d.   Major risks and issues and how the team is addressing them

    e.   Recent accomplishments

    f.   Planned next steps

101. Meet regularly, one-on-one, with your project sponsors. Do not accept that a project sponsor is too senior, too busy, or too disinterested to meet with you. You are managing an initiative that may directly affect the sponsor's annual compensation. Speaking with him or her one-on-one will provide you incredible insight into why the initiative is deemed important. Do this on a regular, appropriate basis.

102. Use a presentation to demonstrate your strategy for the project and to highlight your plan. A presentation is not a project plan; rather, it is a communication tool to provide a broad overview, usually before a detailed project plan is created. Think of the presentation as a sales pitch intended to win support for you, not the project. You want your audience to trust and believe in you, the project manager. You want them to see you as a worthy custodian of the project deliverable.

103. Pay attention to your language during meetings or status reviews. Take care to avoid crutch phrases such as "you know," "basically," "literally," "like," and "um." Don't use pregnant pauses in your dialogue or your hands to make points. Such behavior demonstrates a lack of experience with public speaking—a skill no successful project manager can do without.

General Communication Tips

104. Project management is a specialized craft, much like law, medicine, and construction. Professionals are focused on a discipline with a unique nomenclature, universally accepted definitions, and an endless variation of styles to accomplish a similar goal. If you call yourself a project manager and, more importantly, make your living as a project management professional, dedicate your time to learning the language, definitions, theories, and governing rules of project management to ensure that your unique style is based on universal practices.

105. When assigned as the project manager, take pains to personally introduce yourself to as many project participants as possible. Look each person in the eye and let him or her know you are assigned the responsibility of managing the project. Ask if there is any particular concern the participants immediately have. Provide them with your contact information (e-mail address, desk phone, mobile phone) and ask them to contact you with any questions, concerns, issues, or new information.

106. Project change is an absolute. Prepare for it, accept it, and communicate it when it happens.

107. If you must criticize a project participant, remember to keep the criticism constructive and always criticize the behavior, not the person.

108. Project data, in order to maximize effectiveness, must be synchronous, timely, accurate, complete, and available to everyone who will benefit from the project deliverables.

109. Make it a habit to read news, both internal and external, regarding the company you work for. Search for articles on upcoming reorganizations, financials, changing business philosophies, or any other information that may affect your project, resources, or team dynamic. An excellent online resource for company news is www.glassdoor.com.

110. Establish a clear line of communication that enables team members to report risks and issues. This will reduce confusion and enable your team to quickly learn the system. You can simplify the process for your team by eliminating layers under the governance model, ensuring the most direct path to important issues and risk.

111. Make certain that your resources do not fear open and honest communication with you. Monitor your team on many levels to ensure that sudden changes in responsiveness or delivery are not due to a new task or responsibility assigned by another manager outside the project.

112. If you receive a voice message, respond with a phone call. The person leaving the message may want to offer you information that is best relayed verbally.

113. Remember to say "thank you" often and ensure your project participants understand your genuine gratitude for their hard work and commitment to the project's success. Communicating your appreciation to the team demonstrates that you acknowledge their efforts and value their contributions.

114. Whenever possible, use industry-standard terms and indicators. The chances are you will reach a broader audience with widely accepted nomenclature than if you

use very specific terms that may only apply to unique company, geographic area, or team.

115. Inevitably, a project manager is required to chase team members for information. When requesting an update, perhaps for the third or fourth or tenth time, phrase your request carefully, especially when you need the information. Rather than sending an abrasive or accusatory note, ask if the person needs more information to satisfy your request.

116. Don't assume the members of your project team will govern their actions in the same manner you will. No matter how long the team has been working together, it's prudent to stay closely connected with them, even if you're convinced they know precisely what to do.

117. Sooner or later, someone connected to your project will do something that truly angers you and challenges your ability to control your temper. In such circumstances, remember that you always have the right to be angry, but not the right to be cruel. Avoid harsh treatment of others, especially when you are upset. Always ask yourself, "Am I getting mad for the right reasons?"

118. There will come a time when you must make a critical decision regarding the direction of your project. In most cases, such a decision can be appropriately escalated to your manager or project sponsor, but eventually you will need to make a call on your own without the luxury of escalation. When you find yourself in this situation, remember to first pause and reflect. Attempt to remove all influences of emotion from the situation. Drop any notion of pride and seek counsel when possible. Assemble facts in written form—writing down facts is an exercise that introduces clarity and perspective. Once a decision is reached, stick

with it and remain committed, but never so rigidly as to reject necessary change based on new information. Leaders know there are times when they must revoke their own decisions based on new information. Never surrender your right to be wrong.

119. The title "project manager" is synonymous with "leader." Like it or not, your job is to lead the resources connected with your project to achieve an objective. There are many leadership styles and theories. You should explore as many as possible until you find the one, or the composite of many, that will work best for you. Remember to continue evolving your style, enhancing your best practices and improving your shortcomings. There is, however, one methodology that consistently works, no matter your leadership style: directly telling people what to do. In fact, most resources prefer a clearly communicated directive over the opportunity to figure out the proper course on their own. If you can master the art of telling people what to do in a manner that does not alienate you from them, you are likely to make more progress in a shorter amount of time.

120. There are times when you can communicate too honestly, and this can hurt or help your cause. As a general rule, craft your communications to ensure that you don't invoke unnecessary alarm or provide unnecessary details that may embarrass others or harm reputations. When you are too honest, people may think you disingenuous. Knowing what to reveal, how to reveal it, and when to reveal it are skills that are developed over many years and best aided by experience and error. Two cases highlight the different effects of too much honesty.

Case Study: Too Much Honesty

James, the very technical lead on a software deployment project, was well positioned to lead a group of developers toward a major release of new software code that had more functionality than its predecessors. The release was highly anticipated and just two months away. James felt the pressure but loved it. He was confident in his abilities and those of his team. He knew the new version would be a big hit.

Others in the organization, however, were not as confident. Since the whole company had a lot riding on this release, there were many nervous people, including the company owner, Justin. One day, Justin called a meeting to get a status on how things were proceeding. He thought this would calm everyone's concerns and keep the team focused.

At the meeting, James presented his update with complete confidence. After he finished, there were no questions raised by anyone. The group moved on to the next update, leaving James feeling as though his report had made his job seem easy.

When everyone was finished, James spoke up and said, "There are a few things I think everyone should know." He proceeded to say that his team was working around the clock to ensure that they hit their deadlines. "In fact," he said, "some of them are skipping meals and taking time away from their families. It's been a lot of supervisory work for me, but I'm doing what's needed to hit our dates." Nothing James said was untrue, but the way he characterized it made it seem like there was more to worry about than there truly was.

Once the team was alerted to the pressure on the development team, changes were made to relieve it. These changes involved taking some responsibility away from James and putting more management talent in place. The perception became that perhaps James was in over his head. After all, when other managers got close, they could see that things were under control. If James couldn't see this, maybe he wasn't the manager they thought he was.

In another illustration of too much honesty, Natasha, a senior project manager, found herself managing several projects at once. Although they had a common theme, keeping on top of them with the proper degree of mastery was challenging.

Rather than accept the impossible and doom herself to failure, Natasha walked into her manager's office, sat down, and told him without hesitation or equivocation, "I think you are a terrible program manager and are not doing a good job at all." She proceeded to articulate the effect of having too many projects to manage and the need to spread the responsibility among more team members.

At the time, she probably expected some sort of punishment or retribution. Little did she know that her manager gained a tremendous amount of respect for her that day and took steps to ensure that she was well positioned for success going forward.

Natasha used her experience and acumen to prevent herself from heading for certain failure. She summoned the courage to bluntly tell her manager where she stood. It paid off, both in the short and long terms.

121. In most cases, as project manager, you will find yourself the most broadly knowledgeable member of the team and the one with the greatest insight into the risks, options, and dependencies that will bring in the project on time and within budget. This doesn't mean you are the smartest resource on your team—there are differences among intelligence, education, and awareness—but nevertheless it carries an important responsibility. Resist the temptation to use your superior insight to make other team members feel embarrassed or uninformed, especially your manager. Take special care not to allow your manager to feel as though you have a greater command of the project than he or she does. In circumstances where it is obvious, phrase your statements to appear that you are reminding, not informing, your boss.

122. Learn to separate the important from the trivial. It is useful to define and constantly update your critical path so you may dismiss the unimportant and concentrate on the most essential aspects of moving the project forward. Every project resource will think their work streams are the lifeblood of the project. When issues arise, it's easy for team members to believe the sky is falling. Likewise, it's easy for you to get pulled into this distracted thinking, especially

if you are not constantly refreshing your familiarity with the critical path and the tasks on it. But don't do anything to discourage your resources from thinking their work streams are essential; it will keep them on top of their game.

123. Often it's easier to ask for forgiveness than for permission. Savvy children know this very well and employ it with instinctual accuracy. During the course of your project, circumstances may call for breaking a rule or two, such as escalating an issue to a senior individual to provoke a long-awaited and critical decision. If you ask your direct manager for permission to contact a very senior individual, you are likely to be refused for a variety of reasons, not least the implied negative reflection on your direct manager. If you break the chain of command without asking first, and secure the needed direction, you may infuriate your manager. However, you may also lift a burden from his or her shoulders and therefore receive forgiveness for the transgression. If you ask and are denied, then you may not proceed. But if you proceed without asking and then secure results, you may get forgiveness. Knowing your environment, the politics that dictate the circumstances, and the personalities of the people you are dealing with will help you understand when it is best to seek permission or forgiveness and allow you to act appropriately.

124. Data alone is not enough to help senior managers understand the essence of a project or situation. As the project manager, it is your responsibility to understand the flow of information as it evolves from data to interpretation and ultimately into intelligence. Data is usually comprised of raw facts such as metrics and numbers. Interpretation distills the message that those figures suggest. Combining the message with present and future circumstances develops the intelligence that one can base decisions on. Failing to

understand the differences among data, interpretation, and intelligence, especially when involving senior managers, risks leaving a recipient with the annoying burden of trying to interpret the data on his or her own. You are paid to master the information. Take advantage of your opportunity to help your manager and stakeholders by interpreting the data into actionable intelligence before presenting it.

125. Utilizing the latest technology—smartphones, tablets, laptops, text messaging—is the cost of doing business for a person whose job is to be available twenty-four/seven. A smartphone or tablet is a great tool to ensure that information always remains at your disposal. When working on a large project, travel (even from one floor to the next) is essential. Staying connected is mandatory. Invest in technology solutions that allow you to remain connected, even if you must pay for that investment yourself.

Case Study: Purchase Your Own Equipment if Needed

A program manager at a global organization was hired to bring structure and maturity to a portfolio that was plagued with missed deadlines and poor planning. Henry was seasoned, intelligent, and accomplished, with a long history of success in the field. Recognizing the need for frequent travel to meet with the project team and stakeholders, Henry asked his boss, the project management office head, for a laptop to ensure his ability to remain productive and connected while traveling or in remote locations. His request was refused, based superficially on a lack of demonstrated need. Despite his disappointment, Henry kept up his visits and found he was losing valuable time during the commute. As much as he complained, however, he never purchased a laptop himself.

Months later, Henry found he was the last one to learn about critical news affecting a project under his care. His embarrassment and, perhaps, fear for his reputation forced him to use his own money to purchase a suitable laptop. The $2,000 investment had an almost immediate effect on his productivity and attitude. He felt empowered and in control. Reflecting on the months during which he had refused to purchase the equipment, he recognized how he had let his pride and "I'll show her" attitude impact his effectiveness.

Analysis:

Henry was stubborn in his thinking. He wrestled with the dilemma of using his own money to purchase equipment that would help him do a better job for someone else. He felt that the company should pay for the laptop since he was using it to manage their project. This thinking made him less effective for several months.

Lesson:

Eventually, Henry realized that having the right equipment was more important than the price. Paying for the right equipment is a cost of doing business when your title is project manager.

Proper communication is one of the most challenging aspects of your project management career. By developing good meeting skills, a clear writing style, and effective in-person communication techniques, your work and the work of your team will become more effective, more broadly recognized, and certainly more sought after.

Next, we tackle the topic of transparency.

Chapter Four
Transparency

Sunlight is the best disinfectant.
—Louis Brandeis, US Supreme Court Justice

In the realm of project management, transparency refers to the ability of all project participants—including sponsors, stakeholders, team leads, vendors, and all other resources—to maintain a clear view and understanding of the project details as the project moves forward and circumstances change. Creating an environment that keeps all aspects of a project visible is a very challenging mission, but one vital to the success of a project manager.

126. While it is critically important for a project manager to create transparency for stakeholders, sponsors, and senior management, there is an equal need for stakeholders, sponsors, and senior management to create appropriate

transparency for the entire project team, especially surrounding key decisions, changes, and dependencies. It is the project manager's responsibility to facilitate this two-way street. A good leader can only respond to the best information he or she has. If new or revised information is not shared, the results can lead to confusion and delay.

127. Lee Atwater gave us the line, "Perception is reality." This is especially true in the arena of project management. If your project team or stakeholders believe something is true, they will act as though it is true. One of the most difficult aspects of communication is understanding the perceptions of those you communicate with. Nonverbal communication is even more difficult. Your body language—arms crossed, for example, or brows furrowed—is open to interpretation that may not prove accurate. When you do not have the advantage of communicating with someone in person, things get tougher still; you can only rely on what you hear, with no benefit of eye contact or facial expression. Don't sacrifice correct perception for transparency; it's not worth the cost.

128. No matter how good your reports or how accurate your data, if the right people can't see the information and digest it correctly in less than ten minutes, it is likely to remain shelfware that never sees the light of day.

129. When a team member, including the project manager, is reluctant to offer transparency into the finer details of the work, schedule, budget, and/or risk, it is often an indication that something is wrong. No matter what the project or initiative, greater results are produced when everyone connected to the project can appropriately examine progress, issues, risks, and dependencies. Peer review is a powerful tool to help achieve the best effort from everyone,

but make certain to first create the proper environment that will permit peer reviews to succeed.

130. Always carry out your day-to-day duties as though someone were watching you every minute. This approach will serve as a professional compass to steer your actions. As the proverb says, "Honest labor needs no master."

131. Always publish a status report to the person you report to, even if you are not asked for it. A status report can be something as simple as an e-mail or as comprehensive as a Microsoft PowerPoint presentation. Never assume that your manager is adequately aware of what you are working on or the amount of effort required to deliver the results that you do. If the report is not desired, your manager will let you know. If that is the case, it remains prudent to produce the report but not deliver it. It may have value down the road as a historical record.

132. At any point during a project, under any circumstances of progress or lack thereof, be prepared to provide a succinct and extemporaneous synopsis of the project, including its current health (financial and otherwise), accomplishments, and planned next steps. As project manager, your ability to provide this update without referring to notes is an indication of how well you have mastered the project information, including risks, issues, and dependencies. It is a project manager's responsibility to be aware of all project threads and maintain the ability to communicate a high-level status of the project at any given moment. Having superior information will provide an advantage over your peers.

133. Generally, with mature organizational and transparency techniques, a good project manager can successfully

manage multiple projects at once. The key to managing multiple projects simultaneously is recognizing the need to go wide and not deep. The more widely you must manage, the less detail you can concurrently master for any one of the projects. Of course, complexity and other variables are important factors when determining the appropriate number of projects someone can successfully deliver. All things being equal, the more projects you must manage at once, the less detail you can master for each of them, as conceptually illustrated below.

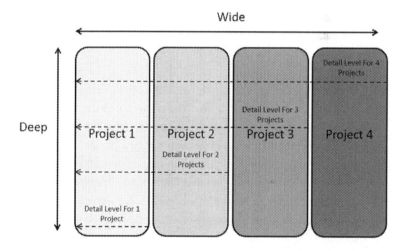

Illustration 1
Limits of Managing Multiple Projects

134. Don't ask anyone on the project team to do anything you are not willing to do yourself, such as work late, arrive early, or complete tasks on your own time. It's important to maintain transparent work habits with your team so they understand what it takes to get the job done. If team members have no clear view of your work habits, they will draw their own conclusions. Habits are hard to start and

hard to break, so make certain you develop habits that will advance your station and influence your team in a positive manner.

135. Everyone recognizes when a team has great chemistry. Strive for it always.

136. Track action items and deliverables using whatever tracking method enables all team members to view open items, ownership, and current status. The more people who see an action item is open—along with its associated owner—the better. Such transparency highlights work that is not yet complete and assists the owner with a clear understanding of what is expected and when.

137. It is very likely, especially in large organizations, that many projects are executing at the same time and drawing from the same resource pools. The more dependencies your project has, the more transparency is needed into other projects and how they are managed. Get to know your fellow project managers and how they operate. A well-organized, well-executed, and well-staffed project can end in disaster if a dependent project is not executed in a similar manner.

138. There is such a thing as too much transparency. Your manager and stakeholders do not require every detail of the project's progress nor about the disagreements that naturally occur among teams. In fact, it is poor form to run every decision you make by your manager. Appropriate transparency provides sufficient information to instill confidence in your ability to manage and exercise good judgment. Regular status reports will maintain that confidence. Significant events, either positive or negative, warrant a break in the regular reporting cycle.

139. Recognize that not everyone connected to your project is as conversant in the procedures and nuances of project methodology as you are. Your project communication may extend to stakeholders well outside the realm of day-to-day operations. If you are aware of anyone connected to your project who falls into this category, invest some time to educate them at a high level. Set expectations about your team, how and why you will employ a certain methodology, and how to understand your status reports. This type of investment goes a long way.

140. Providing sufficient transparency should not compromise other project management duties. A well-structured status report can communicate the aspects of a project suitable for team members, sponsors, and stakeholders. Design your report deliberately and with intent. Be succinct and aware that at any point your report can pass to anyone in the organization. When it does, it should still be a useful tool.

141. Everyone has someone they must answer to. The trick is knowing when you have more than one boss. As a project manager, you usually do, especially when you consider the temporary teams that are formed around projects and the accountability that is due to sponsors, stakeholders, managers, and clients. It is critically important that you identify all the people you are accountable to and understand exactly how they impact the navigation of your assignment landscape, your tenure at the company, and even your compensation. Your direct manager—the one most influencing your pay—should always know where you are physically each workday, what your efforts involve, and any special relationships you have with sponsors, stakeholders, or clients. If you plan a day out of the office, take care to remind your manager (and any others you are accountable to) a couple of days prior to going out, even if

he or she has already approved the time off. This reminder will demonstrate your consideration for your manager's busy schedule and help demonstrate that he or she need not worry too much about supervising you.

Case Study: Who's Your Boss?

During the execution of a strategic project at a Wall Street firm, a project manager, Max, was assigned the task of upgrading the desktop operating system and applications of the firm's proprietary traders, with offices in New York and London. Although relatively few in number, the proprietary group traded the company's own money (as opposed to its customers' money) to make a profit for the firm. Since the group represented a direct impact to the company's revenue stream, they carried significant influence. When it came time to change the technology for these traders, the program's prior track record suggested quite a bit of risk.

Therefore, when Max was assigned, he took the approach of meeting first with the group's senior manager, Robert, in New York and outlining a bespoke strategy that would significantly mitigate the risk and ensure a smoother transition for the entire global group. This strategy cost more, but Max recognized the real cost behind a failed migration or a trader going offline for several hours. The extra effort paid off, and Max soon had the go-ahead to execute the strategy in New York.

Two months later, the New York trading floor was complete, and while there were some issues, none affected the earning potential of a single trader.

With confidence built, Max proposed the same methodology for the London trading floor. Robert stared at him with a puzzled look and matter-of-factly stated, "You'll just go to London and make sure it goes well."

Max called his manager, Denise, and told her that Robert wanted him to go to London to oversee the upgrades of the London trading floor. "Absolutely not," his manager stated. "We have competent people in London, and there is no need to waste money on travel."

The next day, Max informed Robert that he didn't have permission from his manager to travel to London.

Without hesitation, Robert asked Max to accompany him to his assistant's desk. Robert opened his wallet, put his personal American Express card on the desk, and asked his assistant to book Max on a first-class flight to London and a week-long stay at a posh hotel. After the arrangements were made, Max asked Robert if he was sure he wanted to pay over $10,000 for him to go to London. "Oh, I'm not going to pay," Robert replied. "Your boss will reimburse me for every dime!"

Needless to say, once Max's manager found out, she was furious, so much so that she made a trip to the trading floor to discuss the matter with Robert. The day did not end well for Denise; it was soon common knowledge that she had lost the debate with Robert in a very public way.

Analysis:

Max went to London and Robert was fully reimbursed for the trip. From that day forward, Max appreciated the fact that he answered to more than one person. Had he recognized this earlier, he could have handled the situation much better.

Lesson:

Max could have helped prevent Denise's public embarrassment if Max had recognized the authority Robert had over him and the relationship that authority formed; it was the catalyst of the episode. Had Max adequately communicated these circumstances to Denise, he might have resolved the situation without escalation.

---

142. If, as project manager, you get the sense your boss is beginning to micromanage your efforts, examine first if you are providing adequate transparency in a manner that satisfies your manager's needs and wants. Without a common definition of transparency, you and your manager will operate in a dysfunctional state that is likely to erode relationships and confidence.

143. Work to prevent transparency regarding the destructive "little things" that add no value to the project and may cause disharmony among the teams, such as rumors and embellishment. Every project is rife with complaint and disagreement among teams. Most often this does not intrude on project progress. Such information is best kept away from meetings, status reports, and formal communication.

In the rare cases that such minutiae affect project progress, do your best to address the situation immediately and shut it down. If it is truly an issue, you must report it as such.

144. Effective leaders are visible and accessible. Remaining visible to your team, sponsors, and stakeholders requires effort and personality. You must present yourself as an engaging person, seeking others out, mingling in a crowd, and displaying an affable and approachable demeanor, even if that conflicts with your natural personality. People like to associate with confident, knowledgeable, and successful individuals. As you build your portfolio of successful projects, your confidence, knowledge, and ability to remain engaging should rise.

145. Don't hide important personal matters from your project team, sponsors, or stakeholders. If there is a situation in your personal life that will distract you from your management duties, it is best to make key people aware of it so the change in your behavior or ability to deliver is not interpreted as lack of interest, lack of skill, or lack of discipline. If the matter is significant, don't fool yourself—someone will notice it. Failing to make the right people aware risks the opportunity to secure necessary help and/ or understanding.

146. As you strive to increase your value and demonstrate the effectiveness of your methods, it will become increasingly likely that senior management will notice and consider you for more important and visible roles. When this happens, you must have someone identified who is capable and ready to assume your position. Without a suitable replacement, you may lose the opportunity to advance. Take pains to openly identify your successor and perform the necessary training and mentoring to ensure his or her readiness. It

takes a very confident and secure person to train someone else to take on the responsibilities of your own job, but it is the mark of a true leader and demonstrates to management your ability to think beyond the here and now.

147. Before you can effectively manage others and drive a team to a common goal, you must manage yourself. Understand the philosophies and methods that work for you, and demonstrate the success of habits that allow you to consistently deliver your goals. Once you can articulate what works for you and why, you can begin to successfully coach others and help them develop their own capacity to manage themselves.

148. Do not lose sight of what specifically changes as a result of the successful delivery of your project. This often overlooked and underreported perspective can provide valuable intelligence to the senior members of the organization. Articulating the details behind the changes your project brought about is a distinguishing characteristic of a senior project manager.

Case Study: What Goes Away?

Tony, a project manager assigned to manage the up-grade of end-of-life hardware for approximately two hundred applications across an estate of approximately 450 servers, was considered especially appropriate for this project. His technical abilities and acumen allowed Tony to not only lead a team of technicians, but participate in the very technical working sessions that designed a new platform that was more resilient and powerful. This strategy allowed the applications to re-side on a smaller estate of servers, thus saving money.

Tony drafted presentations to communicate the ben-efits and merits of the project with the various stake-holders. The finance department had a query. "What about the project's return on investment and the im-pact of the move to the new platform? How will this affect financials?"

Tony was very technical, but also a seasoned project manager. He easily responded, "The cost of 450 serv-ers was X. The cost of the new estate is Y, resulting in a savings of Z."

This seemed pretty straightforward, and Tony went about executing the project. It was not until the proj-ect was complete that Tony—and many others on the team—realized that when he had responded to the finance department's question months earlier, he had failed to account for the savings on items that went away. The understanding the finance committee was looking for was not simply the difference between the two estate costs, but the savings that would be yield-ed by the infrastructure going away as a result of the project.

Understanding what goes away and when, as well as the associated cost of what goes away (and when) paints a more comprehensive picture of how the proj-ect impacts the organization. Don't neglect to account for what goes away as a result of your project.

149. Maintain financial transparency. A good project manager commands a project's financial health. It is a fundamental project management responsibility to monitor expenses and ensure that costs do not exceed or fall far short of the approved budget. Project sponsors must have transparency regarding the cost of the project as it is executed. The project manager is accountable for monitoring expenses and reporting them on a regular basis.

150. The phrase "lies, damned lies, and statistics" has been attributed to Mark Twain, Benjamin Disraeli, and others. It suggests the persuasive power metrics can have. It also suggests how some people use metrics to support a weak argument, leading others to criticize the metrics when these do not support their positions. Use metrics with careful consideration and appropriate support. Publish accurate metrics by utilizing a repeatable process that has integrity and credibility. Regardless of who is collecting the metrics, the method of data collection and reporting must remain consistent.

151. Providing transparency is not always enough. You need to constantly justify your direction to ensure that your team understands the bigger picture. The information you make transparent must equate to meaning; information without interpretation is not transparency. Albert Einstein said, "Any fool can know. The point is to understand."

152. *Dependence* is defined as the state of needing something or someone else for support or help. In the domain of project management, a *dependency* is the relationship between different project activities, such as tasks, milestones, and action items, to other project activities. Project dependency can also extend to other external projects, vendors, or anything that is required to advance your project.

As shown in illustration 2 below, projects can have dependent relationships to one another. When your project is dependent on another to begin or move forward, this is known as an *upstream dependency*. In similar fashion, if another project cannot begin or move forward until your project completes, this is known as a *downstream dependency*.

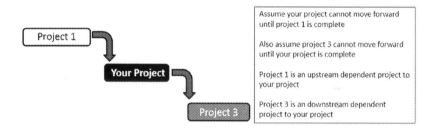

Illustration 2
Project Relationships

Put equal emphasis on providing transparency to your project's upstream and downstream dependencies. This is especially important when you manage a team through a matrix relationship. If there is clear understanding of what impacts your project and the impact your project has on others, teams will have a greater appreciation for the importance of the deliverable.

153. Transparency is best demonstrated by teams working together.

154. You can't maintain transparency and delegate to someone if that someone doesn't know what's going on. Take the pains to ensure that a lieutenant on your team is well prepared to substitute for you with minimal briefing. Doing so will position you to take a vacation, convalesce if needed, or seek a new role with support of senior management.

155. Flexibility is essential for any project manager. It is always better to bend than to break, so expect and embrace change. Allow your project team to witness your adaptability and your positive welcome of change. It will inspire them and decrease anxiety, which is so often a distraction to project execution. If you have not read John Kotter's book, *Our Iceberg Is Melting*, buy it, read it, and keep it on your nightstand.

156. Remain accessible, even on the weekends and during holidays. Make certain everyone can reach you at any time. Publish your mobile phone number and e-mail address so everyone on the project knows how to reach you. This may appear like an invasion of your private time, but the need to be accessible comes with the job of project manager.

157. "Act as if" is a concept every project manager must fully understand and implement, but one that is often lost. As a leader, your job is to alter the status quo, even if that means seeking the slightest bit of improvement. In the absence of overriding direction, assume you are in charge, assume you must make the decisions, and always assume you are responsible for the outcome. This mind-set will help you maintain control.

158. Every person is a valuable asset, though at any given point some are more valuable than others. You never know when you'll need to rely on the janitor to remove a trash can from your path. The person who reports to you today may be your manager or project sponsor tomorrow. Treat everyone with respect and dignity, no matter what their present positions may suggest.

159. The Peter Principle was an observation by Laurence J. Peter and Raymond Hull in a 1969 book of the same title. Peter

and Hull observed that in a hierarchy, employees tend to rise to the level of their incompetence. Another interesting theory is the *halo effect*, developed by psychologist Edward Thorndike in the early twentieth century. It suggests that one's judgment of a person is influenced by an overall impression of him or her, perhaps due to a certain characteristic. It is not uncommon to come across someone on the project team who has been promoted based on a specific characteristic, or promoted to a point where he or she can't add any additional value. For this reason, don't blindly assume everyone in senior management is good at their jobs. You are likely to come across a senior manager who simply isn't bright or effective, yet commands a title and position that you must respect. This is not always easy to navigate, but holding true to certain realities can keep you out of trouble. Always remain respectful. Don't look to throw anyone under the bus. Knowing what you are dealing with is usually enough to determine how best to deal with it. As the saying goes, a disease known is half cured.

160. If you find yourself in a situation where you are presenting information or leading a meeting and you are asked a question that you do not have the answer to, simply state, "I don't know, but I will follow up and get back to you." It is perfectly acceptable not to have the answer to every question. Assuming you have demonstrated your intelligence and capability already, it is better to be sincere and direct. Your audience will appreciate it.

161. No matter the extent of your efforts to provide complete transparency to your project team, stakeholders, and management, they are the final judges of your achievement. Regularly ask if they have enough transparency regarding the project, its dependencies, the risks, and the issues.

More than likely, they will express a desire for more transparency, but don't let this discourage you; stakeholders and management rarely believe they have adequate insight. When confronted with this, simply ask for their suggestions. Allow them to tell you exactly what information they would like and how they would like it in order to satisfy their needs.

Transparency is a crucial element of project management. By keeping staffers, stakeholders, and management in the loop on all aspects, you'll enjoy greater flexibility and less pushback.

Next, we discuss governance and its impact on project management.

Chapter Five
Governance

Plans are nothing. Planning is indispensable.
—Dwight D. Eisenhower

Governance can mean many things to many people. In the perspective of project management, *governance* refers to a set of standard practices, procedures, rules, definitions, and nomenclature that everyone within a team, logical unit, business area, or organization agrees to adopt. The benefit of a governance model is standardization, which permits everyone to speak the same language across different businesses, departments, or geographical regions. A well-defined governance model also permits project managers and team members the ability to move from one project to another with seamless integration. Learning curves are reduced, and fewer project managers can handle more assignments with greater efficiency.

162. A project management office (PMO) is not necessary for every organization. Depending on the problem(s) or the goals of the organization, a formal PMO may not prove the appropriate answer. The purpose behind a PMO is not to track projects or police the actions of the project managers, but to ensure that there is structure and governance behind project execution that allows continuous improvement of delivery in repeatable fashion, and therefore offers predictability. It is important that the PMO mirror the culture of the organization to make certain that the methodologies and best practices support the accepted approach of the company leaders. A PMO without the authority to enact change, drive policy, and maintain a standard will not have a good chance at success. When evaluating the need to establish a PMO, carefully consider the following points:

- What is important to the organization?

- What specifically is the PMO intended to achieve?

- Do company leaders support the intended goal of the PMO?

- How will the PMO align within the organizational structure?

- What magnitude of change will a PMO introduce, and is the organization ready for such change?

If it becomes clear that the setup of a project management office is the right thing to do and that the vision is supported by senior leaders, then adopt a methodical strategy to create an effective PMO.

- Appoint someone who can focus 100 percent of his or her time on the construction and leadership of the PMO. A PMO is a strategic endeavor and requires commitment from everyone involved, especially senior leaders. A PMO needs a leader at the helm.

- Assess the organization to determine which type of PMO is necessary. Depending on the immediate circumstances, the PMO may need to begin with a tactical mission, such as the administrative oversight of a portfolio of work, and mature over time into a supervisory body that challenges the project teams to do better.

- Creating a PMO is a project. Therefore all aspects of successful project management are required, including a business plan, a project charter, a communication plan, a launch plan, a schedule, dependency management, risk management, and resource management.

- Concentrate on quality rather than speed. The creation of a PMO will bring about change, which some may greet with great excitement, especially in the beginning. Maintain a pace that allows each step toward the goal to be rooted in excellence.

- Focus on the team. A successful PMO is built on the foundation of good people working together with a shared vision for success. The PMO leader must invoke commitment and transform a group into an effective team.

- Stay organized. As the PMO is built, several activities must be executed in parallel, such as assessing the team, understanding the tools, developing procedures, and keeping management informed. Organization is the best way to stay abreast of what is important and sustain a productive journey toward the goal.

163. Developing a complete project governance model can take some time, perhaps over the course of many projects or years. However, documenting the outline of a governance model is necessary and appropriate for any project. Some of the fundamental aspects of a governance model are listed in appendix A.

164. A project schedule is not a project plan. Microsoft Project creates project schedules, not plans. Project plans and project schedules are two different things that serve two different functions. Both are living documents that constantly change throughout the life cycle of a project. A project plan articulates the complete approach the team will take to accomplish the project's objective, taking into consideration all of the necessary methodologies and tactics required to control the project. A project schedule is simply a list of tasks with associated dates (duration), dependency information, and ownership. A project schedule is a vehicle used to understand when specific tasks must take place to keep the project on schedule. A project schedule is very useful to understand the critical path and the cascading relationship between tasks and the project completion date. Both a project plan and a project schedule will evolve as the project does. Some of the fundamental elements of a project plan are listed in appendix B.

165. Risks have not yet happened. Issues have already occurred. Every active risk requires a response, and only one of the following is acceptable:

a. Avoid

b. Mitigate

c. Accept

d. Transfer

Once a response is identified, a response plan is required to ensure appropriate management of the risk until it is realized or no longer influences the project. A risk response plan includes the following information:

a. Risk name

b. Description (What is actually at risk? Usually cost, time line, or quality)

c. Impact

d. Probability or likelihood

e. Risk owner

f. Response

g. Specific efforts to keep this risk from being realized

Risk management is one of the most important aspects of project management. No matter how formal or informal your governance model for risk management is, maintaining a consistent methodology is critical to your success in staying ahead of risk impact.

166. Risks, issues, and dependencies are each different, but all require significant focus and appropriate response to keep a project under control.

167. Usually, organizations classify their work in two ways: (1) maintenance of day-to-day operations (keeping the lights on), and (2) efforts to solve a particular problem or achieve a new level of functionality. When an organization or business unit decides to take on work outside day-to-day operations, it's either because it wants to or it must. When it must, this is known as a *mandate*. A mandate could be driven by any number of factors, including a regulatory requirement, a safety issue, or a security need. When an organization wants to solve a problem, gain greater functionality, or increase its competitive edge, senior management typically identifies an initiative to accomplish the goal, and a project is created to address the initiative. In the case of truly big or broad initiatives, especially those that are global in nature, it may take more than one project to accomplish all of the intended results of the initiative. When several projects share a common goal, a program is commonly formed to allow economies of scale and consistent methodologies. It is important to understand the relationships among the different drivers that create work so that you can appreciate how the pieces fit together. Although not all organizations share common terminology for initiatives, mandates, programs, and projects, many apply a hierarchy to distinguish the appropriate management and reporting of each.

168. If the company you work for has a global reach, you should represent your projects and programs from a global perspective, even if you are not assigned to the global project manager. If someone else is assigned to represent the projects and programs globally, it will prove helpful

to him or her to understand your global perspective and properly incorporate it into the reports.

169. Know that your current organization may not adopt certain best practices, such as developing formal project plans, charters, or closure documents, but this shouldn't encourage you to drop these habits from your routine. Once you adopt a project management procedure that works and is proven to add value, stick to it, even if the documents you create are put in a drawer and no one ever reads them.

170. Process is a big part of project management. If the organization you work for already has a defined or mature process for work in and affecting your projects, follow the existing process, even if you believe it can improve. If you recognize a series of actions that can benefit from a defined process, propose one. But no matter whether a process exists or not, remain consistent in your approach to get things done.

171. Each morning, develop a to-do list. Invest ten minutes in organizing the items you must get done and the items you would like to complete. Make this a habit. Creating a to-do list each morning will guide you to a more productive day. It will save you time and sanity. Throughout the day, check off items as you complete them. At the end of the day, review your accomplishments and the items that must be transferred to tomorrow's list.

172. Regardless of the project, there is always the possibility of "scope creep" and requests to make significant changes in deliverables and dates. All such changes must flow through a change control process that is orderly and identifiable as the single method to implement change. Make certain to include in the approval process both senior management

and those who will ultimately implement the change. This will ensure that thorough consideration is given to the consequences of the change. Make certain that a change control process is well documented and communicated among all who may participate or are affected.

173. Part of your ability to effectively manage a project is gaining the trust and respect of your team members. This will come, in part, through your efforts to standardize processes and procedures so everyone operates in a consistent manner. It is likely that some may initially complain about the change in habits, but once instituted, standardized processes will instill trust and respect, and you will recognize the fruits of your labor.

174. When attempting to create a project schedule or update action items, do not accept "maybe" as a valid answer. Expunge "TBD" from your project lexicon. While "I don't know" is a very legitimate answer, it should always follow with a date for the date. Follow up and demand a definitive answer. "Maybe" implies that the respondent does not know and is unwilling to say so. Issues are usually hidden behind phrases such as "I'm unsure" or "I'll get back to you." If someone is struggling with the prospect of providing you the status of a task he or she owns, make things easier by working one-on-one with that person until you can secure the information you need.

175. In order for an action item to be legitimate, the owner must agree to take the action. If there is no one in attendance who can legitimately own the action, assign it to yourself. After the meeting, seek out the correct person and reassign the action item—with the new owner's agreement, of course. If that person does not agree to take the action, seek an alternative resource. If the action requires a resource with

a specific skill set or talent, and he or she will not agree to accept the assignment, simply raise it as an issue for broad discussion at the next status meeting.

176. It's important to structure regular one-on-one meetings with individual team members. Make this part of your governance process. You will quickly benefit from these intimate discussions. The meetings need not run long—fifteen or thirty minutes, perhaps. They also need not remain formal. The value of a meeting is judged by its effectiveness in moving things forward. Meeting over coffee, lunch, or a walk outside on a nice day is perfectly acceptable. The key is to make one-on-one meetings part of your management routine. One-on-one meetings are also a great way to give courage to the timid and help team members discover their talents.

177. When dealing with a difficult resource who must provide you with project updates, try to involve that resource in discussions—especially with senior individuals to whom you are accountable—as to why those updates are important. This change in perspective is often all that is required to secure ideal participation.

178. Throughout your project, remind your resources how their timely updates correlate to milestones and project deliverables. While it may be clear to you, dependencies and delivery times are not always clear to others. It is not uncommon for resources to miss the thread that ties all components together. After all, their jobs are to focus on the details. It is your job to focus on the big picture. You need to remind them often.

179. Print and keep for future reference all testimonials and kudos related to your project management style and

methodology. Collect them as trophies as you move from project to project, even within the same organization. You will certainly face varying degrees of opposition to your suggestions for improving communication, accountability, transparency, and control. Your governance model may come under fire, but if you keep testimony of how your model added value in other projects, new team members may permit you more latitude and acceptance. Use these references as tools, not to brag, but to demonstrate your past value and what you can accomplish.

180. Action items should be due no more than two weeks out. Anything with a greater duration is more appropriately placed on the project schedule.

181. If a project is unpopular, seek out several project sponsors to endorse the project goals. If you cannot find a sponsor to endorse the project goals, it's a clear indication that you must adjust and develop a strategy that compensates for the unpopularity of the mission.

182. For active governance, each project requires a minimum of three types of meetings, each with a different purpose and audience. The frequency of these meetings is provisional, but the necessity to keep them separate is critical. The following are the three meeting types:

    a.   A status meeting

    b.   A team meeting (or working session)

    c.   A planning session

The *status meeting* provides the stakeholders and sponsors with the status of project progress. It is typically thirty or sixty minutes long (depending on the number of work streams) and is not meant for protracted discussion.

The *team meeting* provides an informal venue for the project participants to discuss project problems and delivery obstacles. These meetings are usually specific to a discipline or functional group. It is in this meeting that project schedules are verified or changed to comport with the realities of the circumstances affecting the project.

The *planning session* is the forum used by the project manager to align project schedules, critical path, dependencies, risk management plans, and issue tracking. It is also the forum to gather other project leaders and/or a program manager to ensure interdependent projects have proper transparency to one another.

The typical agenda for a status meeting is as follows:

a. Risk and issue review (project manager)

b. Action item status (open or closed). Do not venture into the reasons behind the status. Otherwise you risk turning your status meeting into a working session.

c. Work stream 1 status (work stream lead 1)

d. Work stream 2 status (work stream lead 2) and so on for all pertinent work streams

e. Other business, or the opportunity for anyone to suggest an agenda item for the next meeting or to highlight other items critical to the status of the project.

The status update provided by the work stream lead should remain limited to the following points and require, in general, no more than ten to fifteen minutes to provide this information:

a. Overall health of the work stream (red/amber/green) and the reasons behind the status

b. Major accomplishments over the past week (or since the last status meeting)

c. Issue report

d. Risk assessment or report

e. Planned next steps between this report and the next status meeting

f. Status commentary (a general assessment of the work stream lead's impression of the project from his or her perspective)

A working session is the gathering of subject matter experts and interested parties to collaborate on a specific project issue, risk, dependency, or direction. A working session may take hours or days to complete, but once complete, a brief status on the resulting decisions is all that is required to update the broader group. Senior management and sponsors rarely need to know how the sausage is made; they simply need to know it is ready to eat.

183. When taking up management of a project in midstream, if the plan or schedule is outdated or simply wrong, take the pains to update each so they are accurate. You will add little value if you do not clearly set forth the true objectives of

the project, along with accurate, published time lines and expectations for delivery.

184. Often, resources have too much on their plates and require management to prioritize their tasks. The resources assigned to a project often have day jobs to concentrate on in addition to project responsibilities. With such pressure, resources may lack the focus to prioritize their workloads. As the project manager, it is your responsibility to meet with the management of your assigned resources and clear their participation in the project. Do not leave this to your resources; their loyalties are to their managers. An inability to prioritize is not necessarily an indication of a poor resource. If left unchecked, however, lack of prioritization is an indication of a poor project manager.

185. Avoid drafting the project schedule for a project you are not managing. Once you agree to draft the schedule and therefore take responsibility for its accuracy and thoroughness, you own the plan and its subsequent evolution. If asked to draft a project schedule for a project you are not assigned to manage, politely offer to assist, but only in a supporting role to the assigned project manager.

186. Publish a mission statement for large or complex projects. A mission statement is a brief and effective description of why the project exists and what it will accomplish. It is not necessary to create a separate mission statement publication; it is perfectly acceptable to include the mission statement as part of the project plan.

187. If an effective system to manage internal and external dependencies is not available to you, do your best to institute a system, even in the most basic form. Dependencies can sink an otherwise well-run project.

Case Study: Going Back to Basics

In 2008, at the height of the global financial crisis, Dean, a well-respected and competent project manager, found himself in a situation that simply didn't make sense. Despite employing the very best practices with regard to methodology, accountability, and communication, the circumstances of the global financial crisis made all the rules, and the rationales attached to them, seem meaningless. Worldwide uncertainty, coupled with draconian measures to preserve capital, made project management much more of an art than a science. People at all levels simply didn't respond as they normally had in years past.

For example, despite the fact that Dean had secured approval to purchase new equipment for the project, when it came time to submit the purchase order, the manager who had previously approved it allowed it to sit on his desk for weeks. He didn't deny the purchase, but he didn't make the effort to move forward either. He left it in limbo as a response to the uncertainty.

In another example, Dean required a decision on hiring a subject matter expert to assist with the project. Although everyone agreed on the need for such a resource, Dean's manager delayed the decision over and over. Dean felt frustrated because he just wanted to know, one way or another, how to proceed with his planning.

After weeks of frustration, Dean was perilously close to paralyzed ineffectiveness, exasperated by his inability to cut through the delays and focus people's attention on the matters at hand. His epiphany came when he read the bestselling book, *In Defense of Food*, by Michael Pollan. Quite remarkably, the book's idea of going back to the very basics of what humans should eat (more plants, less processed food) allowed Dean to realize the benefit of a return to the most fundamental project management practices that almost all others are built on.

The next day he began an examination of the project's critical path to understand precisely what was needed to keep the project on track, within budget, and within the desired quality parameters. Dean created a decision tree that illustrated the impact of each decision (or its delay) on the project deliverable.

By dissecting each milestone, he forced the senior managers to recognize the impact of delay and therefore made it clear that the lack of a decision was indeed a decision to delay, which carried significant consequences. Dean was careful to stick to the facts and avoid hyperbole, which allowed him to present a very matter-of-fact assessment of inaction and its consequences.

When senior management realized that their inaction was actually a proactive decision to delay, and that cost could increase or quality decrease, the necessary people got together to discuss the tough decisions. Their approach avoided putting any one's job on the line because of a single decision.

Dean didn't achieve success in every aspect of the collective uncertainty, but what did emerge was an ability to gain his footing in one of the more significant economic storms of the last eighty years.

The lesson to learn is that going back to basics is sometimes a good strategy. This can apply to everything from the governance model to your leadership style.

---

188. If the terms *WBS, EV, critical path*, and *PERT* are not familiar to you, purchase a book that explains project management nomenclature and make certain you master the terms. As a project manager, you must have familiarity with the terminology of the industry, even if you don't use those terms very often. *Mastering Project Management* and the *Fundamentals of Project Management*, both by James P. Lewis, are excellent resources for learning the language and structure of project management.

189. General Dwight David Eisenhower said of the D-Day invasion of 1944, "Plans are nothing. Planning is indispensable." Adopt this as the creed underlying your daily routine.

190. If you are assigned to be the global project manager, recognize this as a compliment and accept the trust that accompanies such an appointment, along with the responsibility. Prepare to conduct meetings outside your normal workday hours and time zone, accommodating those around the globe when necessary.

191. In almost all cases, it is best to leave a red, amber, or green (RAG) rating subjective. The purpose of marking something red or amber is to communicate the need for help. Use a formula-based RAG rating only in the rarest and

most carefully considered circumstances. When reporting, especially a status report, the RAG rating for project health should consider the perspective of the person sponsoring the project and not always that of the organization executing the project.

192. When drafting a project schedule, ensure that you implement version control. If you have access to a document collaboration tool, such as SharePoint or Documentum, utilize them to keep historical versions of your schedules. Absent any third-party tools to help you maintain independent historical copies, save your schedule with a unique name and date each time you update it. This will ensure that you're able to recover from any mistakes. It will also help prevent team members from accidentally making an update or change that you are not aware of or don't approve.

193. In your project schedule, it helps to rename the column "Finish Date" as "Planned Finish." Then insert a new column and name it "Actual Finish." This will ensure that you accurately record the planned start and finish of each task (your baseline), as well as the actual start and actual finish. This will come in very handy at the end of your project when you begin to author your close-out documentation. It also helps to quickly determine those tasks that are late, allowing you to focus your efforts on them.

194. In your project schedule, rename the "Predecessors" column as "Dependencies." This will make the relationship clearer to your project resources, especially when you utilize the start-to-start, start-to-finish, and finish-to-start options.

195. In your project schedule, rename "Resources" as "Owners" and assign only a single person to each and every task. Don't assign a team. If no single person is assigned as owner and the task runs into issues, you will lose precious time trying to determine the appropriate resource to follow up with. Before assigning a resource as the owner of a task, ensure that the resource agrees with the assignment and responsibility associated with ownership. Absent this agreement, you will lose credibility and accountability for your tasks.

196. Keep on hand and up-to-date a summary of your project plan (Microsoft PowerPoint usually provides an excellent vehicle) to pass along to sponsors or stakeholders who begin to ask the fundamental questions well after the project has begun.

197. A governance model can evolve and should have the agreement of the team that will adopt it. No matter how simple your governance model is to begin with, it's important to document it and keep it up-to-date as the practices expand and evolve. Teams will benefit from participation and will promote new ideas if they are part of the process.

198. A project charter is an important tool that serves to announce a new project and validate the authority of the project manager through the support of senior management, including the project sponsors. There is no need for a complex or verbose document; you can satisfy the requirements of a charter on one sheet of paper. An important note is that different organizations utilize a project charter in different ways. Some see it as a statement of work while others define it as a document that explains the project, its goals, and its purpose. In any case, it should

legitimize the authority of the project manager and the efforts of the project team to begin executing the necessary tasks to achieve the project goal. A good practice is to ensure that it is signed or otherwise formally acknowledged.

199. Always have a working pen and notebook on your person so you can write things down. Make carrying them part of your personal governance model. Choose a notebook that doesn't allow you to easily rip out pages, that is small enough and light enough to carry everywhere, and that is conservative enough not to draw unnecessary attention. Choose a good pen, one that costs a bit more than a standard disposable pen; its value will help keep you from losing it. Besides serving as a vehicle for impromptu notes, messages, or journal entries, your notebook will present an image of fastidious organization, professionalism, and mastery of information.

200. When a project ends, whether well or disastrously, it is a good idea to create and publish a formal closure document that tallies the project's components, such as the following:

   a.   Statement of project objectives and deliverables

   b.   Resource review

   c.   Timescale review

   d.   Budget review

   e.   Ongoing considerations

   f.   Findings and recommendations (including what the project manager did well and could improve upon)

g.   Project exit statement

Project governance involves establishing a set of agreed rules and standards to report progress, track tasks, align resources, and communicate the moving parts of the process. Establishing a clear governance model will help you maintain project control, which we discuss next.

Chapter Six
Control

The time to repair the roof is when the sun is shining.
—John F. Kennedy

From the project management perspective, *project control* is the ability to ensure that necessary action, whether corrective, remedial, or mitigating, is taken at a time that permits the project objectives to stay on track. Addressing an issue or risk too late may require a significant change to the project schedule, the project budget, or the quality of the project deliverable. Project control is not the absence of issues and risk, but the ability to respond to them without jeopardy to the project objective.

There is another aspect of project control that is less recognized but also very important, and that is the ability of the project manager to determine what is in his or her control and what is not. Too often project managers waste precious time chasing issues that are beyond their control. When this happens, a vacuum is left, and the ability to control is actually lost. Understanding what you can control and what you cannot will help you maintain a firm grasp of your project, as well as your confidence.

201. Project control is the output of a good governance model coupled with adequate transparency. In the case of project management, project control is the ability of those in charge to take the necessary action when it is most helpful. You can have transparency and governance, but if the mechanics of the project structure don't allow management to take action, then there is no control. It is similar to receiving a well-written letter from a friend who says he's in trouble and needs help, but doesn't state where he is or how to get in touch with him.

202. The practice of tracking a project or multiple projects by using a spreadsheet exclusively offers no control whatsoever. In fact, what spreadsheets create is a false sense of control. A spreadsheet is a quick-and-dirty scrapbook that produces an instant representation of what's desired. The minute that spreadsheet is shared, all control is lost. False security not only grows, but is spread to a greater population. No one is immune.

203. Escalation—moving up the chain of command to resolve an issue or secure a decision—is an important tool for anyone in the corporate world. It is especially useful for project managers to help ensure that their mission is delivered on time and within budget. It is critically important for project managers to know how to appropriately escalate, as well as to understand the different types of escalation that are appropriate for different objectives.

Before you escalate, understand first why you are escalating and therefore what you want to happen as a result of the escalation. In the realm of project management, there are many reasons to escalate, but the most reoccurring themes focus on escalated matters like these:

a. Securing a decision the project manager is not authorized to make

b. Making senior management aware of a situation, with no action required on their part

c. Making something happen that is not within the power or authority of the project manager

d. Resolving team conflicts that are beyond the authority of the project manager to mediate

e. Forcing the participation of a resource

Common sense states that issues are best resolved at the lowest possible level. Therefore, much skill is required to correctly escalate a matter and secure the desired results without long-term negative consequences. When escalating, ensure that it is the right time to escalate; raising a matter too soon or too late can disqualify the result you want.

Make certain you escalate after you exhaust your capabilities and options to resolve the matter. It can reflect quite negatively on you if you escalate a matter to your boss and she or he tosses it back, expecting you to resolve it.

Once you determine there is no other option and escalation is indeed necessary and appropriate, take care to maintain prudent guidelines.

- Escalate only to a person who can produce the results you want. Ask yourself before you escalate, "Is this the right person?"

- Escalate to the proper level of authority. If you go too high or too low, you risk either a need to re-escalate an issue or the irritation of a senior manager because, in his or her opinion, the matter could have been resolved lower in the management chain.

- Escalate issues in a manner that is helpful to your cause. Clearly state why you are escalating, what you need, when you need the result, and what the escalation is expected to yield. Recommend solutions and remain open to alternative resolutions. Point out possible drawbacks or adverse effects of the escalation.

It is a good idea to close the loop with the person you escalated to. Let him or her know how things turned out and that you appreciate his or her involvement. Reinforce the value the escalation had to move the project forward, thus ensuring that no one doubts your judgment with regard to escalation.

Escalation is a tool you should employ very sparingly. Overused, it reflects a negative image of you.

204. One cannot succeed as both a technical resource and a project manager, although there is the valid concept of a *technical project manager*. The idea here is to determine the role you are best suited for and then draw on your technical aptitude to help manage a project or draw on your project management skills to advance your technical contributions. It's rare and unlikely that someone can perform as a hands-on technical contributor (fingers on the keyboard) and a project manager with mastery of the big

picture. It may seem tempting to jump in and take control when you have expertise in a specific area, but ultimately this will create a false sense of control, as you will leave one role or another vacant.

205. When examining your resources and their project load, don't rely on metrics alone to tell the whole story. You must factor in complexity and seek to include the percentage of time each resource is devoting to his or her projects each day. This will provide a view of the effort required by each resource and a clearer indication as to when and where more resources are needed. Too often, inexperienced program managers attempt to impose a generic workload standard, such as four projects per project manager, and expect this configuration to succeed.

206. As a project manager you will not always have the opportunity to participate in a project at the very beginning (i.e., when it is simply an idea or concept) and follow it through to closure (when the full outcome of the project's effect takes shape in the organization). Most organizations don't realize they need a seasoned project manager until chaos is feared or widespread. Don't use this situation as an excuse to compromise any of your best practices.

207. To assist with project control, if necessary, print the important pages of the project plan and distribute them at meetings. This will enable the team to review the original objectives and identify gaps. You will likely gain valuable insight into risks and issues by reminding everyone of the original objectives. This practice assists with controlling scope creep and is an effective means to solicit feedback.

208. If a project sponsor wants to change the scope to include new and perhaps major deliverables, simply notify the

sponsor in writing of the consequences of expanding the scope. Consequences are not always bad, but they always have impact. If the sponsor formally accepts the well-articulated consequences (including financial consequences), thoroughly document the request and the sponsor's acceptance. Move forward with accommodating the request once it is well communicated and understood by the entire project team. If anyone outside the project wants to change the scope, follow the same procedure, but make certain to obtain documented approval from the project sponsor before implementing any change. The approval document should always include the consequences of the change.

209. Don't allow others to intrude excessively on your time without an appointment. While it is important to remain accessible at all times, if you fail to establish guidelines that protect your time, you will soon find yourself working beyond ten hours a day and falling behind on your minutes, preparation, meeting appointments, and general constitution. Be accessible, but don't let others take advantage of that accessibility.

210. There is no such thing as change without impact to one or more of the following:

   a. Risk

   b. Quality

   c. Cost

   d. Schedule

Case Study: The Business Cards

This lesson was first learned by Mickey long before he became a professional project manager. In college, Mickey was a disc jockey and enjoyed playing private parties and events. At one such party, he was approached by a man who was the general manager of a New York City nightclub. The manager asked Mickey for a business card, but Mickey didn't have one. Embarrassed, he told the manager that he would drop one off the very next day.

The next morning, Mickey raced to a local printer (this was long before the advent of personal-computer printing) and spoke to an older man behind the counter. "I need really good business cards right away," Mickey said with a hint of panic in his voice.

The old man calmly asked him, "How much do you want to spend?"

"As little as possible," Mickey responded.

Without saying a word, the old man took out a piece of paper, drew a circle on it, and divided the circle into three sections. He put a Q in one section, a T in the second, and a C in the last. He showed it to Mickey and said, "Pick any two you want." Mickey was mystified.

The old man went on to explain that the Q was quality, the T was time, and the C was cost. He could make Mickey really nice business cards very quickly, but it would cost a lot of money. He could also make him really nice business cards that didn't cost a lot, but it would take a couple of weeks. Finally, he explained that he could make inexpensive cards right away, but they would not be very impressive. "So," he repeated, "pick any two you want, but you can't have all three."

The following illustration is what the old man presented to Mickey. As simple as it is, it is sometimes useful to demonstrate the *triple constraint* and help a requestor visualize the impact of a change. At any one time, it's possible to maintain control of two constraints at once, but the third requires compromise.

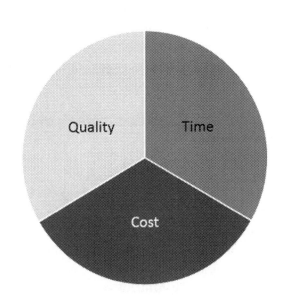

Illustration 3
The Triple Constraint: Time, Quality, Cost

211. Most project planning fails because the project team doesn't have a constructive context in which to discuss risk and proper response.

212. Project deliverables are recognized much faster when the project team can work together with tools everyone is comfortable with and will actually use. This permits greater focus on tasks and leaves the endless paperwork behind. Consistency is key.

213. Don't assume or allow yourself to believe that you work in a stable environment with little to no change, no matter how long a stretch of stability you enjoy. Change is a constant. Sooner or later the world you operate in will shake with seismic force. Prepare for change and embrace it.

214. Respond instantly to false and obvious doomsday threads or discussions. If left unchecked, such negative messaging could capture the attention of your project sponsors. If that happens, you risk losing control of your project.

215. Understand and be prepared to articulate the changes a successful (or unsuccessful) delivery of your project brings about. While these may seem obvious to you, your team, the stakeholders, and the sponsors, they are not always well understood by the broader population. For example, what changes? How are budgets impacted? How do roles and responsibilities change, if at all? What is there now that wasn't there before, such as functionality or convenience or automation?

216. When drafting a project schedule, it is important to lock it down and baseline it to ensure that you have something to measure against as the project moves forward and changes are introduced. It's beneficial in the planning stage to make

119

clear to your team when you will lock down the planned dates. This will help drive team members to focus on the time line they intend to submit.

217. When writing your project plan and/or statement of work, it is equally important to list the out-of-scope items as it is to document the in-scope items.

218. To simplify the communication of risks and issues and maintain control over your project, establish a central and easily accessible online database for reporting them. In your project plan, publish a definition of what a risk is and what an issue is. Also, include your expectations about how team members will update the central repository of risk and issues.

219. Your project will go through cycles of minimal risks and issues and then an onslaught of Murphy's Law. Take care not to waste the time when problems are scarce; use it to review your plan, dive deeper into issues and risk, further communicate with stakeholders, get closer to your project resources, or update schedules to determine opportunities to improve performance.

220. The major challenges you might encounter while managing a project will likely fall within one of these categories:

    a. Resources

    b. Estimating

    c. Budgeting

    d. Authority

e. Control

f. Risk management

g. Reporting and communication

221. Well before your project plan or schedule is ratified and has a baseline, you will circulate many drafts to solicit feedback and comments, thus ensuring buy-in from your entire project team. When distributing draft documents, make certain they are marked as such, quite conspicuously, and that you are specific in your requests to readers that you desire their feedback on the content and direction.

222. You may come to a point in your project when things are just bad. For any variety of reasons, the project may hit a roadblock that impacts morale, evaporates motivation, or fills the future vista with doom and gloom. You may suffer a crisis of confidence or feel your grip start to slip away. When this happens—and it may surprise you to learn just how often it happens and to whom—you must resolve to change course (and perception) by taking bold action. It may seem counterintuitive to promote a courageous course when in the middle of a confidence dilemma, but this is exactly what will help break your bad cycle. Recall that you are often judged by your response to problems and not by the problems themselves. If possible, take a short vacation and use the time away to reflect on your reboot. Or schedule an after-work outing with the team to allow everyone to blow off steam and come together in a social setting to vent ideas. Most importantly, determine the root of your problem, especially if it is you. Take the necessary steps to regain your footing and orient yourself as the person in charge with a clear action plan. As the project manager, it is your responsibility to not only determine the

necessary course correction, but to address the morale and motivation issues with the project team.

223. An attempt to exercise too much control over the many aspects of your project may have an undesired outcome. The Pareto principle, coined by Joseph Juran after the Italian economist Vilfredo Pareto, is more commonly known as the 80-20 rule and states that in many circumstances, 80 percent of effects (problems, risks, issues, etc.) come from 20 percent of the causative agents. This reminds us to continually focus on what truly matters and not get distracted by things that don't matter. If, for example, 80 percent of your project delays can be attributed to 20 percent of the resources assigned, you are better served focusing on the resources causing most of your delays. The proverb "Don't let the perfect be the enemy of the good," which is attributed to Voltaire, highlights the practical impossibility of achieving perfection in any given venture. Take care not to get lost striving for a perfect solution at the expense of an acceptable one. Make peace with imperfection.

224. Don't neglect to record nonbillable or unpaid time you devote to your project. It may never come up, but you certainly want to understand the true effort involved with the delivery of your project. It will help you plan future projects with more accuracy.

225. To best understand where your project stands at any given time, make sure you understand the relationship among four important considerations:

    a. Your goal

    b. The amount of money you have left

c. The amount of time you have left

d. The amount of risk you are in a position to respond to

226. A possible consequence of success is complacency. Resources will let things slide in the knowledge that they can rely on a good project manager to come along and remedy the situation. Take this into account and ensure that you remind resources of their responsibilities. If you permit your resources to constantly rely on you to resolve their issues, you will become overwhelmed and unable to resolve the more critical problems facing the project, which often require more time and dedication to fix.

227. If asked to perform a scope change or other project activity that at first appears contradictory to your efforts, take the time to examine the request. Often a request may seem wrong at first blush, but prove worthwhile after thorough examination.

228. Develop your time lines first through conversation with your team and resources. Then meet individually with each of them to verify the collective output. This will allow greater control over the initial planning and save valuable time.

229. In status meetings, when obtaining updates regarding overdue action items, drive each action item owner to indicate (1) the specific date when he or she will complete the item and (2) a specific reason why the action item is not yet completed. Do not permit the owner to submit a long explanation or excuse surrounding the failure. The objective is to determine if there is a specific problem that you as the project manager are not yet aware of and that is prohibiting the successful completion of a task. Quite

often, the reason behind an overdue action item is that the resource was assigned another task by another manager, perhaps even his or her direct manager. If there is an issue of competing allegiances for your resources, it is best to discover it early and address it.

230. If your project has an issue, report it as soon as your evaluation is complete. Depending on the size of the issue's impact, it may prove prudent to alert the sponsor and senior management right away, with the understanding that you, as the project manager, are assessing the situation and will provide options as soon as possible. In other cases, the best course will be to investigate an issue more thoroughly before reporting it. Knowing your resources, the project's critical path, and management's threshold for information will help you determine the proper course.

231. Understand and appreciate the differences between incident, problem, and change management, and how each might affect your project.

Incident management is the rapid response needed to address an issue that has immediate effect on production and that can damage the organization from a financial, reputational, or compliance perspective.

Problem management is the examination of an incident after it has been resolved to determine the specific factors that contributed to it. Such questions as "Why did this happen?" "What must we do to prevent this in the future?" "What changes are needed to people, process, and/or tools to prevent recurrence?" and "Where else is there such exposure?" are all necessary to ensure not only that the specific incident is avoided, but the broader theme of the incident, such as operating outside standard procedure or the absence of a standard procedure, is not rampant in the environment.

Change management is the adoption of standards that dictate how and when a change can occur, such as adherence to a maker/checker scenario or ensuring requisite approval from the proper people or groups before a change is executed. A documented variance process keeps everyone aware of the protocol to operate outside the standards. Documenting a variance process before it is needed helps demonstrate your forward thinking and eliminates one more thing to do during a crisis.

232. When dealing with external vendors or support contracts, take the time to review the original documents carefully and speak with the account manager. Do not make any assumptions when it comes to support and what those outside your company will and will not do.

233. At the commencement of a new project, or when working with a new team, invest the time necessary to explain your project management style and your standards for meetings, reporting, communicating, and delivery. It is important to let people know what you will stand for and what you will not stand for. Setting expectations up front permits you to overcome the initial resistance that is often found when commencing work with new teams and resources. Enforcing standards will allow the team to adopt them in a spirit of teamwork. Once the team adopts the standards and, more importantly, depends on them, the standards will provide structure to the project, driving efficiency and control.

234. Before taking action, make certain you understand the true nature of a problem. Strip it of emotional noise and the politics that often accompanies bad news. Attempt to isolate the facts. Speak to various parties to gain the greatest depth of perspective. After learning as much as you can about the issue, make an informed decision. This practice

will help you maintain greater control of your project and demonstrate to your team that you are not impetuous. Examine all alternatives and think them through. Write it out on a whiteboard if that exercise helps. Follow through the logical end point of each alternative consequence as you consider them.

235. Make your decisions recognizing that they are provisional, meaning they are determined based on the best information available to you at the time a decision is made. If you secure better information at a later date and it warrants a change in direction, make sure you are the one calling for the change. Don't get married to a direction just because you were the one advocating it.

236. "In the Army, whenever I became fed up with meetings, protocol and paperwork, I could rehabilitate myself by a visit with the troops. Among them, talking to each other as individuals, and listening to each other's stories, I was refreshed and could return to headquarters reassured that, hidden behind administrative entanglements, the military was an enterprise manned by human beings."—Dwight David Eisenhower

This quotation highlights the importance of people and your relationship with them. Ultimately, organizations do not solve problems; people do. Do not lose sight of the fact that it is the relationships among people that gets work done. It is important to build relationships before you need them.

237. A good project manager has many masters. You have to satisfy many people in different layers of management, often with different priorities and conflicting needs. One

who can master the art of service is truly a person of substance.

238. Never exaggerate. It will only ensure the greater disappointment of others when they discover your overstatement.

239. If you attempt to control your project though micromanagement, prepare to deal with a lot of resistance. Generally, good people want freedom to innovate and explore their ideas. Without reasonable flexibility to do so, team members feel constricted, and thus less productive. A demonstration of trust leads to team building, a shared vision, and assurance that the team is always part of the solution instead of the problem.

240. Know the difference between *accountable* and *responsible*. Project managers are accountable for all of the work that must be executed under the heading of a project, but the individual members of the project team (the work streams) are responsible for getting the work done. This is an important distinction to understand and respect, as it can often guide your actions and decisions throughout the life cycle of a project.

241. As your effectiveness grows and becomes more evident, the project team will depend on you more and more. This may seem like a burden and resemble an added responsibility, more like babysitting than project management, but dependence is a powerful tool for control. By assisting others, you can help the overall project move forward with team members who operate with alacrity rather than disdain.

242. The fundamental key to project control is organization. If you can keep all aspects of the project organized and formulate a schedule that permits repeated, effective meetings and status reports, you will master the information and therefore maximize control of the project.

243. "Nearly all men can stand adversity, but if you want to test a man's character, give him power."
—Attributed to Abraham Lincoln

Sooner or later, all of us come across someone in our professional life who is nothing short of a bully. Bullies exert their will as they desire, even when other people do their best to ignore or avoid the bully. A professional bully uses seniority, knowledge, intelligence, connections, tenure, and/or experience to intimidate people and manipulate situations. A bully is unfair. Some people mistake this behavior for passion, but a bully is more likely to prey on others' weaknesses or insecurity. This type of behavior is sometimes exacerbated by the fact that a bully has nothing else in his or her life to moderate his or her outlook; quite simply, the job is everything to him or her. It is, perhaps, the very definition of who he or she is. Any suggestion of not succeeding or winning is interpreted as a reflection of his or her life.

Confronting a professional bully almost never works. Involving the human resources department will almost always result in an undesired outcome for the victim, especially if the bully is viewed as effective or successful by those far removed from the situation. The key to dealing with a bully is remembering that the bully is the one with the problem. Most likely an insecurity of some kind is forcing him or her to overcompensate through aggressive behavior.

Take steps to avoid feeling like a victim. Associate with others who appear immune to the bully's behavior. Empower yourself by demonstrating your abilities in another area; as a project manager, your domain is information across the breadth and depth of the project. Keep a journal to record egregious behavior. Seek advice from someone far removed from the situation.

Depending on the severity of the bullying, you can probably find a way to work around the bully and, despite his or her actions, remain effective in your position. Danger appears when the bully forces you to lose confidence in your own abilities, and you begin to doubt your effectiveness or compromise your actions as a leader. This kind of situation usually results in a self-fulfilling prophecy that allows the bully to claim victory.

A good strategy for avoiding this situation is to recognize the bully mentality and take appropriate steps to guard against the negative impact it can have on you. For example:

- Don't blame yourself. A bully will try to intimidate you into thinking your work is substandard or that you are "not good enough." You must recognize that bully tactics are not about you. They are about the bully. It's a mind game.

- Don't lose your cool. A bully will claim victory if he or she can provoke emotional responses from you and trick you into losing your temper, especially in front of other people.

- Keep a healthy balance between work activities and leisure activities. If you can draw comfort and strength from the various aspects of your life outside of your work (family, friends, hobbies, clubs, and so on), that will empower you to deal with a bully more effectively.

- Above all, remain honest with yourself. Recognize if a particular person in the organization intimidates you or compromises your effectiveness. Despite any tough exterior you may exhibit to your coworkers, you must find a way to deal with the bully and prevent yourself from becoming a victim. The sooner you recognize and admit this to yourself, the sooner you can take the necessary steps, like seeking help, to avoid the consequences.

Project control means more than just keeping track of work. It means creating an environment in which the need for action is understood and the ability to inject that action in a timely fashion is available. Creating the right environment to permit project control depends significantly on your management techniques, which are discussed in the next chapter.

Chapter Seven
Leadership and Style

In any moment of decision the best thing you can do is
the right thing, the next best thing is the wrong thing
and the worst thing you can do is nothing.

—Theodore Roosevelt

Leadership is the ability to influence others, to gain their confidence, and to direct their tasks with their goodwill. Developing effective leadership skills and a leadership style that others will follow with confidence is a fundamental pillar to successful project management.

244. Endeavor to establish a constitution that will govern your actions and help comport your behavior as a means to developing your leadership style. Much of success and failure is rooted in the ability to lead and influence. The style you employ to deliver leadership is just as important

as any initiative you must deliver. A continued investment in leadership training, as well as maintaining the awareness to craft your style with purpose, will complement your other abilities and elevate the value you add. Take time to read about the lessons of others, including some of the world's greatest leaders, and the challenges, decisions, and judgments they faced. Draw inspiration and perseverance from them.

245. Take care not to break your own rules. Team members lose respect for managers who break their own rules.

246. As a leader, you can extend influence far beyond any project you are assigned to deliver. Leading a team includes building a team by teaching and coaching the talent that exists. Growing a team means creating a positive environment that allows people to demonstrate the best of their abilities without fear of rejection, punishment, or failure. If you are recognized as someone who can both lead and grow a great team, opportunities will open for you far beyond project management.

247. If you are just starting out as a project manager or have the ambition to become a better one, seek out a mentor who can guide you. A good mentor can help you avoid many pitfalls and ensure you stay on course. Remember, before you can learn to lead, you must learn to follow. If asked to mentor another project manager, introduce, with enthusiasm, all of the wisdom, tools, and insight that can help achieve success. Remain patient as you demonstrate the best course for your protégé.

248. If asked to mentor a resource, or if you take it upon yourself to mentor someone, you must accept the assignment with the understanding that you are making a serious

commitment, one that requires patience and understanding. Allow sufficient time for your protégé to improve and adopt your teachings. Don't forget that mentoring can teach both parties something new.

249. Adopt a basic set of rules for your meetings. Whatever they are, keep them consistent. Use an appropriate means to enforce your rules and establish your leadership style, such as humor or sarcasm or simple bluntness. Ultimately, your attendees will become familiar with your style and appreciate the consistency.

250. Avoid drinking alcohol with the team. If you must, limit yourself to one drink and then switch to water. It is important to keep your wits about you when in the company of professionals; opportunity and risk are always present.

251. A good leader, and therefore a good project manager, understands that expecting people to follow standards requires people to know and understand the standards that are set. Once people understand what the standard is, they must also understand how they are measured against it. It is likewise important to define a variance process that anticipates and plans for activities that will inevitably fall outside the standard.

252. If you must discipline a team member, do so in private. Take care to avoid the earshot of anyone else, especially an open conference bridge.

253. A good project manager is always aware that resources are often bound to other projects or responsibilities, and not everyone is good at time management. Help as often as you can.

Case Study: Complaining to the Boss

Once, on an especially visible project with lots of dependencies, Bob, a project manager, chastised Rick, a team member from another department, in a meeting. "You didn't deliver the data parameters on time!" Rick could only hang his head and said little in reply.

Bob knew that Rick had other responsibilities outside the project, but Bob took a very myopic view of Rick's performance. Rick went back to his boss, complained, and developed a negative attitude toward the project and its manager, which set the effectiveness of the entire team behind.

Months later, after reflecting on the consequences of the episode, Bob had an opportunity to choose a different course. The next time a team member failed to deliver a task on time, Bob took care to meet privately with that person and ask if there was anything he could do to help get the deliverable completed. This new team member confessed that he was stretched between his project responsibilities and those of his day job, unable to do both successfully.

"Thanks for letting me know," Bob said. He then met with the resource's boss and explained the situation, noting the importance of both the project and the everyday responsibilities of the team members. In a collaborative effort, the two leaders figured out a way to accommodate both needs and permit the team member to feel successful. This course had a direct impact on morale and delivery.

---

254. Take care of your most unpleasant tasks as early in the day as possible. If you don't, you will find yourself thinking about them all day. For example, if you must deal with an employee who is not performing, or worse, must fire someone for cause, make sure it is done early in the morning so you may free your mind to focus on other tasks.

255. In any organization, especially the larger ones, leaders are present in various forms. There are official leaders, those with the title and seniority to direct policy and make decisions, but there are also unofficial leaders. Unofficial leaders are those who may not have the title or seniority of an official leader, but nevertheless are often consulted for advice, counsel, or direction. They are thought leaders, and their leadership manifests through influence. Unofficial leaders are just as important to the organization as official leaders. Seek them out and align yourself with them, even if they seem unpopular at first. If you have not yet earned the title or rank you are striving for, position yourself as an unofficial leader to help pave your way.

256. Don't allow emotion to intrude on your leadership style. While sympathizing or commiserating is sometimes helpful when coaching, you must avoid the opportunity for others to perceive your leadership as fixed in emotional reaction.

257. Avoid judging others based on hearsay. Draw your own conclusions and opinions based on your own experiences and observations. Everyone goes through good periods and bad periods; it's the natural order of how things work. Some

periods last longer than others, but there is no one in the workforce who hasn't suffered a particularly challenging or disappointing period in his or her career. This is true for Thomas A. Edison, John D. Rockefeller, Jamie Dimon, and Steve Jobs, among countless others. What sets leaders apart is their ability to learn from the challenging periods and reinvent themselves better than ever. If you make the mistake of judging people purely on an isolated period or circumstance, you risk failing to benefit from the lessons they learned and that you too can learn from.

258. Attempt to wait a day before granting the request of a team member. Managers get in trouble by too quickly approving a team member's request without taking sufficient time to think the request through. For example, during the execution of a very high-profile, high-pressure project, many team members were forced to work long hours and over many weekends. The toll began to affect the morale of the team. One team member, feeling empowered by his responsibilities within the project, asked the project manager for a bonus, phrasing the request to ensure it was interpreted as a "retention" bonus. The project manager quickly agreed that the critical resource had indeed been a vital part of the project delivery and that losing such a resource would surely set the project back. So the bonus was approved. Had the project manager waited a day, he would have realized that word of the bonus would certainly circulate and that before long, many other critical resources would line up to request a similar bonus. The lesson is to pause before granting what seems like an obvious request, in order to reflect on the possible outcomes.

259. It is the responsibility of the project manager to inform a requestor when what has been asked for is impossible. Don't assume, because it is obvious to you, that everyone

recognizes the impossibility of getting a task done, especially when time is a constraint. While it may seem as though you are disappointing the requestor—and this is especially difficult in a client relationship—setting proper expectations is ultimately more helpful that trying to keep a promise you cannot. As you mature in your role, the value of your word will increase. It takes a single slip of judgment to lose the precious trust you have worked so hard to accumulate. As the proverb says, "Nothing is lighter than a promise, so promise little and deliver much."

260. Anyone who tells you to "just get it done" may not appreciate the value professional project management brings to a situation.

Case Study: The Producer

A company sought to recruit top talent to the firm and hired a television producer, Andrew, at a fee of $50,000, to create a ten-minute promotional video that would highlight the many great aspects of the organization.

Andrew asked his employer, an older gentleman, Mr. Whall, whom he should talk to in order to make the video.

He was given eight names and told, "Just get it done."

Andrew dutifully set off to interview the eight people and spent thirty minutes with each subject, asking them a standard set of questions. Those interviewed had little to offer in terms of promotional material, and nothing jumped out as very useful for accomplishing the goal.

Andrew spent a couple of weeks working with the four hours of footage to create the video. He then invited Mr. Whall to view the raw footage—all four hours of it. What Mr. Whall saw were unmotivated, disinterested, and uninspiring people who had little to say about their company, especially from a positive perspective. Completely disillusioned, Mr. Whall sat with a blank look on his face and finally said, "That's awful!"

Andrew then proceeded to show Mr. Whall the ten-minute video he had created by weaving together only the very best aspects of each person's interview. When properly sequenced and arranged to complement one another, the best of each interview was enough to create an inspiring ten-minute video that precisely hit the mark Mr. Whall was hoping for.

"Why did you have me sit through the four hours of raw footage?" Mr. Whall asked.

Andrew smiled. "I wanted to ensure that you knew what you were paying for."

Mr. Whall gratefully furnished the check, truly understanding the value of what he paid for.

Analysis:

Clearly Mr. Whall was unaware of the significant effort involved in producing a short video that would attract top talent to his firm. Besides being disconnected from his people, he didn't appreciate how difficult it would

A Pocket Guide for Project Managers

prove to satisfy his demands. Andrew knew it would take tremendous effort to produce the ten-minute video, but also knew that making it look too easy would leave his employer questioning the fee.

Lesson:

As a manager and leader, it's your job to translate a request to "just get it done" into a value proposition for your employer. Let the right people know the value of your services.

261. Be confident without appearing cocky. When you issue a mandate, set a standard, make a decision, or chair a meeting, show confidence. Others will notice this and recognize your leadership. If you are unsure in your decision making, others will realize it and be unsure whether to follow you. If you have a crisis of confidence, or have self-doubt that you cannot hide, address it outside the view of the entire project team. A leader cannot succeed without confidence, but a quick way to fail is to be overconfident.

262. Always comport yourself in a professional style, whether it is dress, speech, conduct, body language, or manners.

263. It is wise to dress professionally, above and beyond what most consider appropriate. Simply stated, people react differently to you depending on how you dress, especially those who don't know you. If you look like everyone else, people will treat you like everyone else. Your attire should present you in a manner that highlights your attention to detail. As a leader, you must maintain the flexibility to appear in front of any audience. Most people, without

realizing it, will judge you on your appearance. While it is now commonplace in almost all companies to dress casually at least some of the time, notice how the senior executives outfit themselves and mimic their standards.

264. Take credit for very little. Highlight achievements made by your team and individuals within the team. There is little to gain by publishing to a wide audience what "you" achieved. Over time, the contributions you make by leading an effective team will become apparent. Focus on the bigger picture instead of smaller, individual tasks.

265. Do not succumb to speaking like "one of the boys" (or the girls) when in a group. Avoid the use of foul language, no matter how prevalent or accepted it is. Although others may speak unprofessionally, your job is to stand out and lead, not follow. When you speak and act professionally, people in turn will treat you professionally. It is possible to demonstrate a firm and assertive position without sacrificing your manners.

266. When assigning resources to your project team—or as they are assigned for you—make certain to learn a little bit about each of your team members outside their specific skills. This information may include planned vacation time, commute time to work, responsibilities outside of work (such as coaching a child's soccer team), or religious or cultural observances that may influence your ability to schedule or rely on the resource at a particular time.

267. It is a project manager's job to remind, follow up, nag, pester, and reward team members.

268. The project manager must assume a chief-of-staff role for stakeholders and sponsors. The chief of staff mind-set

helps articulate the responsibilities the project manager must perform, which take great skill and discretion. These responsibilities often include overseeing the actions of the entire project team, managing the project schedule, and deciding which course to follow when critical decisions are required. A chief of staff is sometimes labeled the gatekeeper or "the power behind the throne." When I was asked to describe the chief of staff position to a direct report, this served to convey the spirit:

> As the person I have total trust and confidence in, I want to position you as my filter. I want you to work so closely with me that, in effect, everyone will treat you as they do me. With you I am 100 percent more effective than without you. I need you to reach, guide, and direct me and my team toward the vision I create and keep us all honest and on track, especially as we interact with the other members of the global team. No matter how hard I work or how smart I am, I can't achieve my vision by myself. I always need a trusted advisor right next to me.

> I need you to help me define the functions we require, select the best people for those functions, remove the people we don't need, control the flow of information coming into the organization, adjust it to my style, and manage our message in a way that always brokers honesty, integrity, and support among our customers and colleagues.

> I need your constant advice on direction and decorum. I need your help to protect me from those who want to detract from my vision.

If your boss can see you in this light, feel confident you are on the right track. If you are fortunate enough to find someone whom you see in this light, appreciate the valuable relationship and cultivate it for growth beyond any singular project or endeavor.

269. If you are involved with social networks, keep in mind that anything posted to sites such as Facebook, Twitter, or LinkedIn is potentially available for anyone to see. While it may seem logical to separate your personal time and activities from your professional ones, managers, colleagues, and potential employers may not see it that way, and you may never get the chance to explain.

270. If you have a lot of free time during the day, you're doing something very wrong.

271. If a project manager does the job right from the beginning, the best time for him or her to take vacation is during the execution phase.

272. Compile a portfolio (both hard copy and electronic) of your work, one that includes sample project plans, project schedules, templates for meeting agendas and minutes, and any other artifacts that demonstrate your communication, organization, and leadership abilities. Include testimonials from previous assignments and recommendations from former managers. Compile a list of references who will speak on your behalf. Create a project summary that, unlike a résumé or curriculum vitae, lists only the projects you worked on and what you delivered as a result. These will all help to highlight your command of best practices, demonstrate your sense of self-worth, and provide insight into your leadership style.

273. When you get what you want, stop talking.

274. To lead people, walk beside them . . .
    As for the best leaders, the people do not notice
    their existence.
    The next best, the people honor and praise.
    The next, the people fear; and the next, the people
    hate . . .
    When the best leader's work is done the people say,
    We did it ourselves!
                                                    —Lao Tzu

275. You owe it to the profession to mold new project managers
    and teach them the very best practices of the trade. There
    is little value to junior project managers; either you can
    manage a project or you cannot. If a person has not yet
    mastered the required skills to manage projects, consider
    that person a project coordinator and rely on him or her as
    such. Treat the learner as an apprentice who must practice
    the craft for five to seven years before becoming effective
    as a project manager.

275. Most people do not know how to differentiate between a
    good project manager and a bad one. They often rely on
    credentials, such as the PMP certification, but these can
    easily misrepresent the comprehensive skill set needed to
    deliver a project successfully and lead a team of disparate
    individuals toward a common cause. It is up to you to
    demonstrate your depth and breadth of skills, which
    include the ability to lead. Sometimes a certification is
    nothing more than an indication of the ability to pass a
    test. The PMP alone is not a good measure of a project
    manager's ability, and you should not expect it to resonate
    as such. Allow accomplishments and referrals to guide the
    evaluation of you.

277. If you have not mastered the art of multitasking, you must practice and get better. The very core of a project manager's responsibility is to remain abreast of many things at once. If you cannot do this effectively—and make it look easy— then you may not succeed as a project manager at all.

278. When communicating the value you add, state your accomplishments and *not* your day-to-day activities.

279. Spend an appropriate amount of time outside of work, enjoying yourself or tending to personal matters. This will help you to maintain a healthy balance of work and play, keeping your personal affairs in order so you can ensure that, when you are working, work has your full attention. It is quite possible for the most talented person to become ineffective because of private issues that always seem to take precedence. Find meaning in your leisure.

280. Treat all team members, junior to senior, with the same level of respect. Do not play favorites; you will lose.

281. "Vision without execution is a hallucination."—Thomas A. Edison

282. Maintain contact with resources external to your project whom you deem highly effective. You will likely need to seek their assistance or advice at some point in the future. Highly effective people will always land on a winning team.

283. Sometimes it is just easier to let someone else believe a good idea is his or hers! Remember, as the project manager and the one accountable for the delivery, your true value lies in getting the good idea implemented.

284. When offered advice, listen to all of it and then assess it. There is nothing to lose by considering a different opinion. Even if you don't agree with it, do not discredit it entirely. Rather, solicit the opinions of your other resources, especially those who disagree with you. Listening to advice doesn't mean you have to take it. Don't dismiss a good idea just because you don't like where it came from.

285. Ask questions you don't know the answers to.

286. Discourage most ad hoc requests—even if you can accommodate them—to ensure that others understand that such requests take time and that your time is valuable. It is important to master the art of refusing work. Often termed "push back," a project manager must know when to apply it and when to avoid it. If you are assigned too many projects, with an expectation of zero compromise in the level of management, and you attempt to accommodate such assignments, you will find the only way to succeed is to work more than ten hours a day. It is your responsibility to analyze the situation and present the project sponsors with a plan that permits the success of all projects with a requisite level of management.

287. If you don't enjoy public speaking, or attempt to avoid it when called upon, consider joining Toastmasters International (www.toastmasters.org). Toastmasters will help you improve your public speaking and presentation skills and will certainly help boost your self-confidence. Project managers must do a lot of public speaking. Whether addressing a large audience or simply chairing a meeting, it is all very much public speaking, and the same skills apply to each, especially when your goal is to educate, inform, or persuade your audience. It's an essential leadership skill.

288. Upon completion of major milestones, recognize and praise your team, including anyone else who contributed to your success, by e-mailing the project sponsors and thanking your team. Ensure that you include everyone in the e-mail by compiling a list over the course of the project. Do your best not to leave anyone out.

In some cases, a more pronounced gift of gratitude is called for. In these cases, it is often best to thank an employee by providing him or her with tickets to a performance or a dinner at a very nice restaurant. By doing so, you allow the employee to invite his or her spouse and show off the value the company places on the employee's contribution. Sharing work satisfaction with a spouse is a very rewarding experience.

Interestingly, some believe that paying team members for extra tasks completed actually has a negative effect on their performance, because what they were once doing voluntarily, they now expect to get paid for. For most, satisfaction from work comes from a few factors: (1) the worker believes the wage is fair, (2) the worker believes he or she operates in a climate where the worker has a voice and is heard, and (3) the worker has a certain degree of control over how he or she operates each day.

289. At the start of the new year, write down the professional accomplishments you hope to complete for that year. Review the list from time to time and make changes if necessary, recording the reasons why. This exercise will help you correctly ascertain your capabilities. Take on too much and you'll probably discover you make progress in many areas, but complete few.

290. As much as you can, stay out of office politics! A grapevine grows in every company, and human nature attracts us to it. It is best if you avoid this game altogether. Don't complain about others or express judgment of their performances in a public or private forum. The information or disinformation you get in return can lead to very bad decisions. While people may grow annoyed with your unwillingness to participate, you will always command great respect for your fortitude in remaining above the pettiness. Never subtract from your character to add to your popularity.

291. Success is a horrible teacher. The difficulties and issues you encounter during your project not only help define the type of project manager you are, but serve as a great teacher for your next project. While it is natural to feel bad, discouraged, or disillusioned after a mistake, recognize that such mistakes are what make you better. Don't waste time on regret. When you make a mistake, whether in judgment or assignment, don't beat yourself up or waste time attempting to cover it up or deflect the blame. Meet the mistake head-on and take corrective action right away. Any negative reflection on you due to the mistake will be quickly overcome by the praise that will come with the new direction that puts everyone in good light.

292. "Optimism and pessimism are infectious and they spread more rapidly from the head downward than in any other direction."—Dwight David Eisenhower

293. Do not let it shock you if you suddenly realize that everyone thinks you report to him or her, especially if you require the assistance of multiple teams. For the sake of your project, do not let it bother you or affect your work. You know your reporting line; figure out how to keep your stakeholders

happy without alienating any of them. The least of your concerns should be your ego.

294. Your professional world will always include those who help you and those who wish to see you fail. It is an unpleasant fact that you will not win over everyone. When you encounter someone who doesn't want to see you succeed, or worse, demonstrates malicious intention to make you flop, it is best to keep to the high road. This doesn't mean you cower like a frightened animal; it means you don't sink to the level of unprofessional or rude behavior that could hurt you down the road. Don't tattle. Avoid retaliation. Ensure that you don't offer any pretext for baseless claims. Refusing to engage in the inevitable back-and-forth that accompanies such a situation will help you separate yourself from these individuals and do the only thing that truly works to minimize their effect: make them irrelevant.

295. As a leader and manager, you must hone the sense that alerts you to a rift within your team. When you notice such a condition, address it immediately. Bad or hurt feelings, if left to brew, can derail your project more easily than you may think. In most cases, simply promoting an open dialogue or listening with genuine interest can mend the bruise. Allowing a person to vent is often all that is needed to get back on track.

296. An insult lasts a lot longer than a physical injury. Guard against insulting people, whether intentionally or not. If you do insult someone, intentionally or not, do your level best to mend the bruise.

297. On a regular basis, dedicate time to attend classes that will increase your professional knowledge and sharpen your abilities. This exercise will continually improve your

abilities and help you avoid becoming too comfortable with your skill set. Make others aware of the courses you find valuable. Doing so will further establish you as a subject matter expert.

298. Take time off. If you don't acclimate your team to the possibility (and necessity) of the project manager's unavailability from time to time, you will build yourself into a single point of failure. While this is a great ego boost, it's not the mark of a professional. A good leader empowers and prepares his or her team to carry on despite an absence. Taking time off, with confidence in your team, also allows you to recharge your batteries and demonstrates your ability to maintain an effective team. If you take time off and your team's effectiveness falls apart, you are accountable, not them.

299. From time to time, it is necessary to break a rule. This is perfectly appropriate, but only under the condition that before you break a rule, you know and respect the rule.

300. It is generally accepted that one should never burn a bridge. No matter how difficult you find an organization's culture, a team member, or a project resource, avoid any action that may jeopardize the opportunity to work with or depend on that resource in the future. If necessary, find a graceful way out of a situation that doesn't cast blame or suggest you are a quitter.

301. Don't hesitate to share your templates and methodologies with others who want to use and emulate them. Aside from the fact that imitation is the highest form of flattery, the more prevalent your best methods are in an organization, the more they will be traced back to you.

302. As a leader, you will likely need to evaluate others, whether officially or unofficially. You should likewise recognize that other leaders in the organization will evaluate you. If asked to present a self-assessment, make certain you do so in a balanced fashion. This means you highlight your accomplishments as well as your challenges and areas of improvement. Everyone has challenges or areas that can be improved upon. Presenting a balanced self-assessment demonstrates your self-awareness and helps your manager focus on the areas that trouble you most. No one is without difficulty or stress points, and failing to address them with honesty and integrity only suggests one more challenge to overcome. Knowing your faults is a strength.

303. Do your best to help members of your project team, no matter the situation, no matter the time of day. As your project team learns to depend on you, they will seek your counsel more and more often, which will result in greater insight for you and better opportunity to avoid risks and issues. Whenever possible, extend a hand and remain a source of dependability. The lifeline you throw will pay dividends tenfold.

304. One of the biggest obstacles a project manager may face is the inability to prioritize, whether it involves tasks, reporting, or several projects. You must learn the skill of prioritization. Even when you master it, make it a practice to ask your manager often to assist with the prioritization of your time and efforts, as well as those of the project team(s). Although you may have command of the projects under your management, don't neglect the fact that circumstances outside the realm of your projects may affect or possibly trump your plans. Also remember that your project is not the only source of concern for your stakeholders. Therefore, an issue with your project may wind up as one of several

issues that the stakeholders are dealing with, which puts them in a position of issue fatigue. You may or may not feel the effect of this fatigue, but it's helpful to keep in mind the possibility that your project is just one of many, many things that your stakeholders must worry about. When many of them go wrong at the same time, the situation can change dramatically.

305. When your boss tells you to do something, make it a priority. If your boss tells you to do many things at the same time, ask for priority ranking. Once you have direction, the responsibility is yours to execute. If you believe the direction is wrong, you have a responsibility to bring it to your boss and discuss it. Reasonably report your progress to your boss, whether she or he asks for it or not, especially if execution will take more than a couple of days.

306. Leadership often involves alternative approaches. In general, if you are unable to convey a thought and/or resolve an issue via three e-mail responses, use a different medium. E-mail is an excellent tool of communication; however, it is not effective in conveying and obtaining feedback on complex topics. Instead, utilize other methods at your disposal, such as phone calls, visiting someone's office, organizing a meeting, or having lunch with a few key individuals. Such practice and style is the very best way to remain connected with your project and the people responsible for executing it. Strive to meet individually with team members on a regular basis.

307. A project manager speaks truth to power. Always. You must learn to speak up and act with courage when you think sponsors or stakeholders are taking the wrong approach. If you or a member of your team has a better idea or see the need for a change, formulate your message carefully and

deliver it. You must trust that your senior leaders will not take it personally or take offense. By the same token, when a member of your team feels the need to bring something to your attention, make certain to maintain the environment that allows others to speak the truth to you.

308. Not everyone involved in a particular project is as conversant as you are in the proper procedures and nuances of project methodology. Therefore, others may grow impatient or intolerant of your methods as you try to enforce strict meeting times or chair a work breakdown structure meeting. Investing time to educate team members on the benefit of such methods will go a long way.

309. If you have a very big or sensitive ego, there is a very good likelihood that your work as a project manager will often disappoint you. Do not measure your success by a title, the number of people who report to you, or the amount of money you make. Compensation and promotion are by-products of your achievement and are a measure of the quality of the work you perform. If you remain focused on executing the very best job you can while maintaining a leadership position, title and money will come. Quite often, the real secret to success is doing what you love.

310. Reward those who make the organization successful before making themselves successful. A good project manager can help the two happen at the same time.

311. Adopt a style that allows you to provide your insight without mixing your view with the facts. As project manager, you have a unique position to see and hear things others may not. Sponsors and stakeholders will rely on your thoughts and opinions. Make sure you share them appropriately,

and always make certain to distinguish them from the facts.

312. It is good form to recognize that there are pros and cons to almost everything. If you can keep this in mind, it will assist you to understand the perspective of those who have not bought in to your mission or seem to lack support for your mandate. Appreciation of plural perspectives is the first step in bridging the communication gap.

313. Most senior managers appreciate information top to bottom. This means starting with an executive summary that puts the headline up front; the details then follow. Less is more. Technologists tend to correspond in a language all their own, which usually provides historical data that builds to a logical conclusion. Avoid this technique when dealing with business leaders outside the technology arena.

314. Presentation matters. Know your audience and make certain you know how to hit the mark in terms of what they wish to see and how they wish to see it, no matter whether it is a formal or informal communication. Endeavor to use the language of your audience to be most effective. Avoid tech-speak.

315. Practice the art of briefing. The ability to provide precise instructions or essential information is key to any managerial or leadership position. Briefings are how most senior leaders process information. It takes training to perfect a briefing style, and depending on the audience, the approach may change. Practice the form of a verbal summary accompanied by a single page of necessary details. Measure your progress by your ability to isolate the most important information and keep the message to

a single page. The lack of follow-up questions from your audience is a sign of progress.

Case Study: "This is business. Not personal."

Tom, a well-respected and competent project manager with a long track record of delivering complex projects, found himself thrust into the management of an assignment that was midstream in its execution and suffering from a long history of mishandling. There was so much blame to go around that many, from junior workers to senior managers, felt relieved that the eventual outcome could well qualify as an institutional failure and not the direct result of a few individuals' actions or inaction.

Tom knew just what to do. His experience provided a comfortable disposition to deal with the chaos. He immediately met with the project sponsors and convinced them that he needed a month to assess the situation and determine the proper course to get the project on track. He recognized that project leaders and technical staff were disconnected in communications and accountability. Tom highlighted the need to replace certain technical work stream leads with either more competent individuals or individuals with the proper attitude to get the project completed. Tom learned that the poor execution of the project had caused many to disassociate themselves from involvement, which led to relaxed accountability, missed deadlines, and increased risk. It was a self-fulfilling prophecy that Tom had to decisively recast. Tom's effectiveness was rooted in his confidence that senior management supported him and supported the need for change.

Fast-forward eight months, and the outlook for the project was much different. The changes Tom put in place improved the course of the project and the outlook of the entire team. There were some rough spots, and at times Tom was certainly not popular with some project participants. Looking at the big picture, however, success was now a likely outcome. Those still connected to the project basked in the sunlight of contribution and achievement, despite the rocky road and protracted time line.

At the end of the project, with the celebratory e-mails distributed and the congratulatory party ended, Tom put the final touches on the close-out documentation: a complete review of the project and its outcome. It included lessons learned, ongoing considerations, and financial impact. Tom noted the lack of technical leadership at the project's inception and the lack of accountability among management and technical staff.

The review, while perfectly on point and without assignment of any blame or finger pointing, was interpreted by many as an indictment of senior leaders for not ensuring that the right mixture of expertise and management were properly engaged. Many in senior positions felt the embarrassment of a mishandled project, despite its eventual success.

Just as Tom was reflecting on his success and looking forward to his next assignment, his manager called him into his office. "Why did you publish this project review?" the manager asked sternly.

"Well, it was intended to help prevent a repeat of the sinking project I just rescued."

His manager shook his head. "Not from my perspective. That report highlighted the disastrous state of the project before you took over and cast a very, very unfavorable light on those in charge at the time."

According to the review, certain leaders in the organization had failed to take action as the project spun out of control. Perhaps most egregiously, those same leaders distanced themselves from the project rather than take any action to correct it. While Tom did not intend to embarrass anyone or call attention to the ineffectiveness of the leaders, his published document did exactly that.

The senior team at the heart of Tom's review had no intention of shouldering blame or supporting the idea that they had failed to act appropriately, but they had no choice but to acknowledge the points Tom put forth. So, in an effort to shield themselves from further criticism, the senior management team chose to focus on one of Tom's points—the fact that there was a gap in common knowledge between the project manager and the technical teams—and highlight it as the crux of the failure. In an effort to further instill confidence in their own ability to control things, management dictated that project managers had to have a certain degree of technical proficiency. Nontechnical project managers were no longer part of the model that would drive greater efficiency, accountability, and results.

In response to Tom's project review, the management team determined that Tom fell short of the necessary technical standard and should therefore move on. It took about three months, but eventually Tom was replaced with a project manager who was a lot more technical and commanded the respect of the technical teams. Tom's manager had the displeasure of relaying the news to Tom. It didn't matter that the project management skills were compromised. The new model called for greater interaction among technical teams and those managing the deliverables; it only made sense to have them speak a more common language.

Tom was devastated. He never saw it coming. He eventually found a new job at another company, but never forgot the experience. It helped shape his actions for years to come.

Analysis:

Tom's review correctly pointed out the many failures associated with the project before he got involved. And while his intention was to prevent a repeat of the same situation, the unintended embarrassment he caused required others to defend themselves and distract accountability away from them. Unfortunately, their senior positions allowed them to choose Tom as the scapegoat and used his own review to justify releasing him from the company.

Lesson:

All ranks of people, from junior workers to the most senior managers, have the instinct of self-preservation, which you cannot underestimate. Senior leaders are likely to be older and more seasoned. They often have more to lose when their reputations are tarnished or called into question, which means their actions will be more focused and direct. In Tom's case, he wounded the reputations, and perhaps egos, of the senior leaders. Although they liked Tom on a personal level, they could not allow such tarnish to remain, lest they find themselves explaining their inaction.

When reputations are at stake, most people will do whatever is necessary to protect them, even if it means sacrificing a person whom they like or know is innocent of wrongdoing. As you manage projects, keep careful note of how your style, presentations, reports, and reviews impact the reputations of those associated with the project. Avoid bruising the wrong people.

---

316. Much of your style is woven by your training, personality, tolerance, and empathy. Nothing helps define you as approachable as much as your civility toward others. This includes the basic courtesy of responding, no matter the rank or seniority of the requestor. If asked for something, especially after business hours, send an acknowledgment, even if it simply states that you will look into it or that you don't have the answer. Quite often, an after-hours request is based on an urgent situation. The project manager is the logical place to start. In such situations, the comfort of a simple acknowledgment is enough to diffuse panic and instill reliance.

317. Don't dwell on the past or maintain the false belief that you cannot recover from a serious mistake. When something goes wrong, focus on your response and how to prevent it from happening again. The toughest part is remaining honest with yourself; was it your fault, partially

or otherwise? Did you miscalculate? As you recover, avoid embellishment or reticence that may allow others to draw the wrong conclusions. "If you're going through hell, keep going."—Winston Churchill

318. Make certain to carefully prepare for key meetings and presentations. Orchestrate your meetings down to the finest detail and perform enough due diligence to understand, as much as possible, what will transpire as the participants deliver messages, ask questions, and provide responses. Think of yourself as a courtroom lawyer who never asks a question she or he doesn't already know the answer to. If you can position yourself to know the updates your work stream leads will deliver, it will help you address any questions that come out of the blue and cement your position of master of information.

319. One of the most respected character traits is loyalty. Your project team will depend on you to provide them with the necessary cover when mistakes are made. In situations where things do not go well, don't point fingers. Promote the idea of a team collective, with a need to trust, support, and sometimes defend one other.

Case Study: I Want His Head

Sam was a program manager with several project managers working for him. All the projects involved technology-driven initiatives that made business people very nervous. Business folks know the criticality of properly functioning technology in order to remain competitive.

Sam's project team was a mix of various talents. Each person brought a unique ingredient to the team, and they all relied upon one another for help when it was needed.

During the execution of one particular project, one of Sam's project managers, John, gave the approval to delete some data that the business team had not cleared for deletion. Clearly, John had made a mistake, and there was no easy fix. It didn't take long for the e-mails and phone calls to start.

John became so nervous that he took several walks around the block to try and calm down. He knew this was an offense he could easily lose his job over. As the pressure mounted, John walked to Sam's office, not knowing how to explain. By this time, Sam had heard about the incident, but he had not spoken to anyone about it yet.

"Come in, John," Sam advised. John could tell Sam knew something was wrong.

"This is pretty bad. I have no excuse. I just messed up really bad, and I don't know what to do."

"How big is the problem?" Sam asked.

"I'm not sure," said John. "No one can stop yelling long enough for me to find out. It must be really bad."

"People are attached to their data and very sensitive about it. We'll figure it out," said Sam.

Sam then picked up the phone and called the senior manager responsible for the data that was lost.

"What in God's name happened?" the manager shouted.

Sam remained very calm and in a polite, composed tone said, "Someone made a mistake and the data was lost. We will try to get it restored from a backup, but there are no guarantees, and it may take a few days."

"Who made the mistake? I want his name. No, I want his head! This is so unacceptable! I can't begin to believe we let someone work here who would make such a stupid mistake!" screamed the manager.

"It doesn't matter who made the mistake. It was a member of my team, and it was a mistake, one we can possibly rectify. Before we ask for anyone's head, let's understand what we can do," said Sam in the same tranquil tone.

"I'm not going to wait. I don't want to wait!" yelled the manager, even more irate than before. "I want the name of the person who made the mistake. Period!"

"I'm not giving you a name," Sam said. "If you want a name, take mine. It's my team and I am responsible."

The manager slammed the phone down without responding.

John sat in silence as he looked at Sam. All he could say was, "Thank you."

Analysis:

Before Sam met with John, he knew about the data loss. He also knew John very well and understood no one could punish John more than John himself for the mistake he had made. Sam also knew the manager affected by the mistake. This manager was a bit of a hothead, so Sam expected some over-the-top reaction.

Sam correctly provided John the cover he needed to weather the storm. Sam knew it was exactly what John needed to remain an effective member of the team. The data was eventually recovered from a backup and in much less time than originally anticipated. Once the data was restored, the manager forgot about his quest for a head.

What remained with John from that day forward was the loyalty Sam had shown him during a very uncertain period. That loyalty inspired John, and the lesson remained with him far longer than the project, the job, or the company.

Lesson:

As a project or program manager, it is your duty to protect your team members and ensure that they know they can count on you to provide the cover they need, especially in a bad situation. Such situations present themselves rarely, but when they do, it's important to act in a manner that will inspire loyalty and trust. One's true character is revealed during troubling times.

320. A good leader does not accept the status quo. Whether
you are a project manager or any other type of leader,
it is a fundamental ingredient of leadership style to look
for improvement opportunities and design a strategy to
execute them, no matter how overwhelming they may
seem. Endeavor to align yourself with the mouse whose
running shoes are always on, as in the book by Dr. Spencer
Johnson, *Who Moved My Cheese?* Change is inevitable.
Whether you fear it or not, it will occur. Better to be a
driving force of change and steer its execution than to react
to it.

321. If you are placed in a position to manage a team of direct
reports, make certain you have a clear understanding of the
work habits that are acceptable to you and those that are
not. For example, some managers don't mind employees
working from home several days a week. Other managers
only permit working from home once a week or only on
Fridays. You don't want to wait for a member of your team
to ask for a work arrangement to decide if it is acceptable
to you. Nor do you want to find yourself in the position of
wishing you had never granted permission because suddenly
you find it doesn't comport with your management style.
You must also consider the consequences for the entire
team. You can't afford to appear to be playing favorites. It is
best to understand, as a manager, what honestly works for
you and what doesn't. You can then confidently direct your
team in a consistent and effective manner that won't leave
you questioning your style or regretting your decisions.

322. Some people are just not meant for project management.
A good and effective project manager combines practical
knowledge, command of applied practices, and people
skills that permit a flexible, dependable, and controlled
style. It typically takes seven to ten years of experience

in various circumstances to master the delicate balance of authority, knowledge, and communication to truly demonstrate effective project management.

Leadership and style are additional tools in your project management toolbox. Taking the time to develop your leadership and management style, along with your own techniques, will serve you and your projects well.

Toolboxes also need tools, the topic of the next chapter.

Chapter Eight
Tools

The smallest good deed is better than the grandest intention.
—Jacques Joseph Duguet

There is no silver bullet for project management. Managing a large, complex initiative is a skill that is developed through years of experience and highlighted by battle scars from judgment errors, mistakes, and bad choices. Even the most effective tools in the world remain merely tools. While a hammer is effective for driving nails, a hammer cannot tell you where to best place the nail. Choose your tools based not on their ability to do your work for you, but rather their capacity to reduce overhead, so there is more time for team members to interact on a personal basis with each other and you.

323. Effective project management tools have the following characteristics:

a.   Available to all

b.   Easy to use

c.   Fit for purpose

d.   A proper repository for collaborative effort

324.   Useful tools are flexible and can accommodate the varying needs of different organizations, such as nomenclature, definition, ranking, and language.

325.   Relatively speaking, don't pay a lot for a good project management tool, but don't assume you can build one yourself that will serve the real needs of an enterprise organization. Finding the right tool requires homework, with in-depth research to determine if the tool will prove effective for a given project in a given organization at a given time. Start with a list of requirements and then match those against the thousands of available tools. Gantthead. com has a very good repository of tools that are indexed by feature.

326.   The proper methodology can work as a useful tool toward your project's goals. There are many methodologies to consider. Each has advantages and disadvantages, depending on the mission you are attempting to execute and the environment you are working in. Understanding the popular methodologies and determining which is best for your particular need is key. Listed here are some of the more popular methodologies (not an exhaustive list) and a brief description of each. There is extensive information available from multiple sources. If none of these seems a good fit for your project or environment, rest assured there are others to consider. And, if for nothing else, memorize

this list for your next interview, to demonstrate your awareness of the broader methods:

- **Agile:** Agile is perhaps the most popular methodology for software development, but is also useful for other types of projects. The Agile method seeks to provide fast, continuous delivery of smaller sets of deliverables to the stakeholder. Agile is not a linear process. Instead, it intentionally avoids defining the end result at the inception of the project, allowing a more flexible approach. This doesn't mean there is a lack of governance. Quite the contrary; Agile has a disciplined process, but the fluid nature of the requirements and their ability to change many times throughout the life cycle creates a more flexible approach.

- **Scrum:** Scrum is a form of the Agile methodology insofar as it is a flexible approach that allows fluid response to requirements that are not finalized. Scrum has its own identity because it focuses on short "sprints" (usually thirty days), during which the team concentrates only on the deliverables of the next thirty days. By rendering invisible the overwhelming, long-term deliverables of the mission, the team is made more productive. There is no concept of a project manager under the Scrum methodology. Rather, there is a "Scrum Master" who coordinates the necessary communication and removes obstacles that divert team members from the mission at hand. Scrum relies on all team members, who are 100 percent dedicated to the project and work in the same physical space.

- **Waterfall:** The Waterfall method is very common and is perhaps the most broadly used across multiple organization types, although it originated in the construction and manufacturing sectors. As the name implies, the Waterfall method employs distinct, sequential phases that follow one another. Each phase has its own deliverables and is dependent on the preceding phase. There are many, many variations of the Waterfall phases. Here is one example:

1. Requirements gathering
2. Design
3. Development
4. Integration
5. Testing (user acceptance, performance, etc.)
6. Production release
7. Maintenance

- **Rapid Application Development (RAD):** RAD is almost always used for software development and minimizes planning in favor of more rapid development of the prototype. The planning element is combined with the development of the software and is intended to permit faster coding with greater flexibility to alter requirements. There are four phases to the RAD methodology:

1. Requirements planning
2. User design
3. Construction
4. Cutover

RAD has its critics, who state that the lack of thorough planning disqualifies the ability to accommodate complex or significant functionality. The advent of the smartphone and simpler applications may allow RAD to gain popularity again.

- **PRINCE2 (Projects In a Controlled Environment, version 2):** The PRINCE2 methodology was developed by the United Kingdom's Office of Government Commerce and is broadly used throughout the UK government as the standard project management methodology. PRINCE2 has also been adopted by many organizations in the private sector. The methodology centers on process and has seven principles, themes, and business cases that define it:

Principles:

1. Continued business justification
2. Learn from experience
3. Defined roles and responsibilities
4. Manage by stages
5. Manage by exception
6. Focus on products
7. Tailored to suit the project environment

Themes:

1. Business case
2. Organization
3. Quality
4. Plans
5. Risk
6. Change
7. Progress

Processes:

1. Starting up a project
2. Initiating a project

3. Directing a project
4. Controlling a stage
5. Managing stage boundaries
6. Managing production delivery
7. Closing a project

- **Six Sigma**: Six Sigma was developed by Motorola in 1981 as a means to improve process. The methodology became broadly recognized and respected when, in the mid-1990s, Jack Welch used it as a pillar to his business strategy at General Electric. Six Sigma is a disciplined process improvement methodology that seeks to improve processes by eliminating defects. Project managers may not view this as a methodology per se, but the themes suggest a commonality with project management. Since the term *Six Sigma* has become synonymous with management and process best practices, there is a natural link to project management. The following are Six Sigma themes:

  - Continuous effort to achieve stable and predictable process results is of vital importance to business success.
  - Manufacturing and business processes have characteristics that can be measured, analyzed, controlled, and improved.
  - Achieving sustained quality improvement requires commitment from the entire organization, particularly from top-level management.

The hallmarks of Six Sigma include these four traits:

1. A clear focus on achieving measurable and quantifiable financial returns from any Six Sigma project

2. An increased emphasis on strong and passionate management leadership and support

3. A hierarchy including "Champions," "Master Black Belts," "Black Belts," and "Green Belts" to lead and implement the Six Sigma approach

4. A clear commitment to make decisions on the basis of verifiable data and statistical methods rather than assumptions and guesswork

Six Sigma projects are executed via a specific set of steps and maintain value targets as success criteria—for example, improve customer satisfaction, reduce expense, improve time to market, and reduce production downtime.

327. As a skilled carpenter does, a good project manager keeps several key tools in his or her tool chest, using the appropriate tool in the appropriate situation. Identify the tools that are useful to you and master them, knowing how and when to use them effectively. Always include Microsoft Office, Microsoft Project, a PDF creator, a recorder, a notebook, a good pen, a watch, and a smartphone. These are essential and serve as a foundation to build upon; they will help ensure you remain as effective as possible.

Case Study: Uncommon Tools

You just never know what tools will prove the most effective for a particular project. In one case, a real estate project manager was coordinating the move of several offices to new buildings in a general area. It was a move from a single office building to several buildings in a campus setting. The project plans, project schedules, risk management, and resources were all top-notch. A Microsoft SharePoint was set up to ensure collaboration among the various teams that needed to stay in sync across the different campus buildings.

Despite having all of the necessary tools in place, and providing the best oversight of resources, meetings, and support, Phillip, the project manager, was unable to capture a rhythm that enabled task execution with tactically sharp precision.

One evening, after a particularly challenging weekend of moves, the team was blowing off stream in a local pub. Phillip was feigning a happy mood. He secretly felt that he was letting down the team because he had not yet thought of an idea to crystallize the efforts of everyone involved. As he sat at the bar talking to a team member, he was distracted by a police officer who entered and sat next to him. The officer's radio was loud and echoed nonstop messages from what seemed like twenty people.

Intrigued, Phillip turned to the officer, who quickly apologized and lowered his radio volume.

"Actually, I'm curious," Phillip said. "What's the purpose of the radio? It sounded like complete gibberish, with everyone talking at once."

"Well, it may sound like gibberish, but the radios actually allow everyone to remain coordinated despite their location. After a while, it's easy to figure out when a call is for you or when you can ignore it."

The next day, Phillip decided to conduct an experiment. He visited a local home improvement store and purchased sixteen walkie-talkies. He handed these out to various teams involved with the project moves and asked them to use the walkie-talkies during the next weekend's move.

To everyone's surprise, the radios proved to be the X factor that allowed everyone to coordinate more effectively. Because the walkie-talkies' range spanned several miles, changes, delays, and issues were communicated in real time, allowing others to react instantaneously. The walkie-talkies proved to be the most valuable tool in the successful execution of the real estate move project. The project manager was hailed a genius for thinking outside the box and arriving at an unlikely solution.

---

328. Post-it Notes are a great tool to help a team understand a work breakdown structure. Gather your team in a room and ask for ideas. Write each idea on a Post-it Note and scatter them on a whiteboard. After the ideas are down, categorize them (planning, execution, and so on) and order them sequentially. Then ask for best-case and worst-case time

durations. Before you know it, you have a work breakdown structure driven by an engaged group. Do this over a lunch session and you will really get broad participation.

329. If the limit of your project management tool set is e-mail and spreadsheets, eventually you will face significant difficulty. Spreadsheets offer the challenge of version control. The minute a workbook is shared, it is out of date. The ease of spreadsheets is infectious and tempts a recipient to add a column or row or filter to make the spreadsheet represent more of what he or she wants. Expand your tool set beyond e-mail and spreadsheets.

330. One of the fundamental tools to acquire—in whichever way is most feasible—is a web-based, accessible dashboard of all project and program activity. A dashboard should present limited data points to all stakeholders at once. In this case, less is truly more. For example, a dashboard could present the following data points:

a. Project name

b. Project manager

c. Start date

d. End date

e. RAG rating

f. Percentage complete

g. Project status (in progress, on hold, terminated, etc.)

h. Last modified.

"Last modified" is extremely important to ensure accountability among those responsible for keeping project information up-to-date.

331. Learn how to use scheduling tool, such as Microsoft Project, in a manner that makes sense to those viewing it. Utilize the columns you can customize and add a RAG rating to obtain wider understanding from your audience.

332. The following are some of the most common requirements for a project management tool:

    a. Web-based

    b. Easy to use

    c. Limit the data points team members need to enter or maintain

    d. Scalable

    e. Customizable

    f. Useful on mobile devices, such as smartphones and tablets

    g. Include proper security

    h. Serves as a single repository for project information that everyone can access at once and is recognized as the "golden source" for project data.

333. The more automated your tools, the more you need to check them. It is easy to rely on a tool that produces metrics or calculates your percentage complete, but take care not

to do so blindly. You are responsible for everything you publish and must have the ability to explain it. Your tools must serve you in this regard. The saying "A bad workman blames his tools" highlights the need to avoid using your tools as an excuse for a poorly managed or delivered project.

Tools—choosing them, using them, and maintaining them—are another critical element of project management. Though the types and varieties will constantly change, the need to implement them well won't.

Conclusion

We encounter project management in much of what we do every day, from child care to home renovation to party planning. Most of us do it in some form without realizing it, but we all tend to notice when it is done poorly by others. Project management is a service, and just like any other service that one pays for, there is an expectation and strong desire for effective execution with professional pride.

Certainly there are different degrees of criticality within project management; the project managers working at NASA face different levels of scrutiny than those planning a birthday party. But common themes hold true. Regardless of the situation, the installation of a project manager carries with it an expectation of organization, ownership, communication, and delivery.

If you shy away from leadership or want to avoid dealing with diverse personalities under stressful conditions, project management is likely not for you.

If you thrive on solving problems, appreciate the challenges that require innovative, critical thinking, and feel comfortable taking charge, sometimes in the face of uncertainty, then project management is a profession you can strive to master.

Above all, never forget that a project manager is first and foremost a leader, expected to maintain a leadership position in every respect.

A project manager is not only a change agent but an innovator. The opportunity to grow as a professional and lead others to more effective and rewarding careers is unbounded.

A work of reflection is not complete without recognizing the tremendous value of failure, especially when such failures instigate learning experiences that carry forward for years to come. The experiences that led me to compile these pieces of wisdom are intertwined with failures of various magnitudes. At one point in my career I switched from feeling embarrassed by my failures to recognizing their tremendous power as learning tools. As Winston Churchill said, "Success consists of going from failure to failure without loss of enthusiasm." I truly believe life is a collection of experiences, and the more you have, good or bad, the more valuable your collection is. Today I am a mentor and coach to many people in my profession. The theme I stress over and over is the good fortune to fail, recover, and learn.

By applying the lessons you've learned here about accountability, communication, transparency, governance, control, leadership, and tools, you'll find that projects on and off the job can run more smoothly and produce better results.

Appendices

Appendix A
Fundamental Aspects of a Governance Model

a. Common Definitions and Acronyms

    i. RAG (Red/Amber/Green) Definitions

        1. Gray = not started
        2. Green = no issues / no major risk / within budget
        3. Amber = minor issues / minor risk / exceeding budget
        4. Red = major issues / significant risk / significantly exceeding budget
        5. Purple = on hold
        6. Blue = complete

        • time (on schedule / behind schedule)

- issues and risk (major/minor)
- cost (within budget / exceeding budget)

ii.   Project States

- open
- closed
- on hold
- change request
- closed
- terminated

iii.   Percentage Complete

- Define the methodology that will calculate percentage complete. Formulas are often a bad idea.

iv.   Regional Areas

- North America
- South America
- Americas
- Europe
- Middle East
- Africa
- Asia
- Australia

v.   Constraint Types

- time
- cost
- quality

vi. Dependency Types

- internal
- external
- other projects
- internal work streams
- outside vendors

vi. Priority Definitions

- critical
- high
- medium
- low

vii. Program and Project Definition

- What makes something a project vs. business-as-usual work?
- What makes something a program?
- Can a program have only one subproject?
- What is the difference between an initiative and a mandate?

viii. Milestone

- Milestones have no duration, but some organizations may permit duration, despite the egregious error.

ix. Project Initiation Process

- Determine if a project initiation process is already in place. If not, is a process necessary? Many organizations vet the need for a project very carefully, but most lack a formal governance model that solicits consistent information and allows an informed decision based on common criteria.

- Typical project initiation information includes the following pieces:

  a. The project's intended outcome
  b. The project necessity
  c. Required date
  d. The necessary investment
  e. Project justification
  f. Project prerequisites
  g. Consequences of completing or failing to complete the project
  h. Project sponsors
  i. Priority
  j. Project benefits
  k. Key vendors
  l. Return on investment

b. Reporting

  i. What is the complement of reports necessary for all staff levels?

  ii. How often are reports published?

  iii. Who publishes reports to the following people:

    1. Team members
    2. Direct managers
    3. Senior managers
    4. Clients

    iv.   Are different organizations competing with each other using different reports?

    v.   Are different reports extracting the same information from different sources?

c.   Roles and Responsibilities

    i.   The role and responsibility of the project management office

    ii.   The role and responsibility of the project sponsors

    iii.   The role and responsibility of project stakeholders

    iv.   The role and responsibility of the project manager. This is especially important if there are multiple project managers assigned to a project across regions.

d.   Cost Centers or Cost Codes

    i.   Who pays for project work under different initiatives and mandates?

    ii.   How is payment transacted among different business units and organizations, or within the same department?

e.   Default Currency

Appendix B
Fundamental Elements
of a Project Plan

A plan typically includes the following information:

- executive summary
- project overview (with an optional mission statement for large or complex projects)
- project objectives
- statement of work
- roles and responsibilities

  ✓ project executive
  ✓ project sponsor(s)
  ✓ project management office lead
  ✓ project manager
  ✓ work stream leaders
  ✓ additional resources

   ✓   escalation procedures

- technical requirements
- assumptions
- constraints
- risks
- dependencies
- client responsibilities
- vendor responsibilities
- working definitions
- project control
- approach

   ✓   prescribed guidelines

- meetings and communication
- issue management
- contingency planning
- project major phases
- major milestones
- project budget
- appendix A—project schedule
- appendix B—technical requirements
- appendix C—project contact list
- appendix D—governance model

Appendix C

Meeting Agenda Template

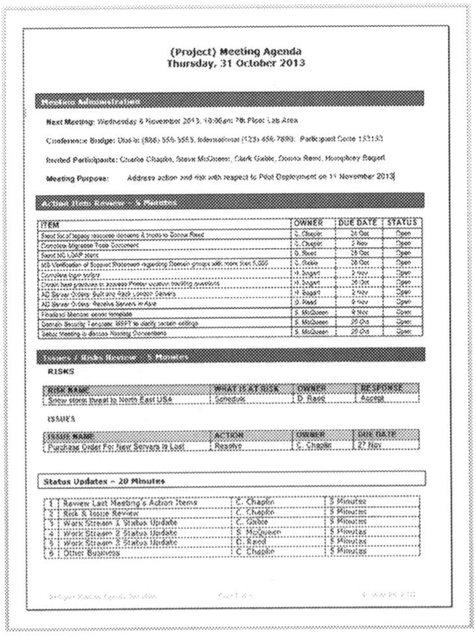
(Project) Meeting Agenda
Thursday, 31 October 2013

Next Meeting: Wednesday 6 November 2013, 10:00am 7th Floor Lab Area

Conference Bridge: Dial-in: (866) 555-5555, International (123) 456-7890; Participant Code 123123

Invited Participants: Charlie Chaplin, Steve McQueen, Clark Gable, Donna Reed, Humphrey Bogart

Meeting Purpose: Address action and risk with respect to Pilot Deployment on 11 November 2013

ITEM	OWNER	DUE DATE	STATUS
[illegible]	C. Chaplin	[illegible]	Open
[illegible]	C. Chaplin	2 Nov	Open
[illegible]	D. Reed	28 Oct	Open
[illegible]	C. Gable	28 Oct	Open
[illegible]	H. Bogart	2 Nov	Open
[illegible]	H. Bogart	[illegible]	Open
AD Server Orders: [illegible]	H. Bogart	2 Nov	Open
AD Server Orders: [illegible]	D. Reed	[illegible]	Open
[illegible]	S. McQueen	[illegible]	Open
[illegible]	S. McQueen	[illegible]	Open
[illegible]	S. McQueen	[illegible]	Open

RISKS

RISK NAME	WHAT IS AT RISK	OWNER	RESPONSE
Snow storm threat to North East USA	Schedule	D. Reed	Accept

ISSUES

ISSUE NAME	ACTION	OWNER	DUE DATE
Purchase Order For New Servers is Lost	Resolve	C. Chaplin	27 Nov

Status Updates – 20 Minutes

1	Review Last Meeting's Action Items	C. Chaplin	5 Minutes
2	Risk & Issue Review	C. Chaplin	5 Minutes
3	Work Stream 1 Status Update	C. Gable	5 Minutes
4	Work Stream 2 Status Update	S. McQueen	5 Minutes
5	Work Stream 3 Status Update	D. Reed	5 Minutes
6	Other Business	C. Chaplin	5 Minutes

Appendix D
Interview Questions for Project Managers

When interviewing for a project management position, here are some questions to ask the organization that is seeking your talent.

1. Is this a new position or is the slot a replacement?

2. If a replacement, why is there a vacancy? If new, why create a senior project management role now? Has something changed in the company?

3. What is management's view of project management? Is there strong backing and proper authority given to the project managers? Are project managers granted the necessary authority to implement change?

4. Is there a formal project management office?

5. Is there a risk methodology in place to properly address risk?

6. Is a project management methodology already in place with senior management buy-in? If so, does it follow Project Management Institute (PMI) standards?

7. What tools are used for project management, communication, and reporting?

8. Am I permitted to bring in my own templates and tools?

9. Is there a central repository for all project-related documentation?

10. Does the company employ matrix management for project resources?

11. Is there a formal process to properly budget projects to ensure adequate resources from inception to final delivery?

12. What was the most successful project in the past year, and what made it a success?

13. How many project managers are in the group currently? Is this the largest or smallest it's ever been? Is the group growing or shrinking?

14. Typically, what is the ratio of project manager to projects?

15. Are the development teams accustomed to independent work, without the oversight of project management

best practices, and therefore reluctant to adopt new techniques and methodologies?

16. How would the introduction of new processes and procedures be received, from the technical teams to the management teams?

17. Typically, I introduce needed change quickly and efficiently, such as running tight meetings and ensuring that action items are addressed. Is there a chance of culture shock, and if yes, how will management react?

18. How supportive is the company when it comes to professional training, books, and the opportunity to attend professional seminars?

19. Does project budget and vendor management fall within the scope of project management responsibilities? If not, who handles these?

20. Does the project management team meet on a regular basis to share ideas and discuss techniques, or does everyone adopt their own methods and practices?

21. Is there a central repository for project information, such as SharePoint?

22. What is the typical escalation path for problems, issues, risks, and critical information?

23. Of all your current project managers, who has been with the company the longest? How many years?

Bibliography

Ambrose, Stephen E. *Eisenhower: Soldier and President.* New York: Simon & Schuster, 1991.

Bunkley, Nick. "Joseph Juran, 103, Pioneer in Quality Control, Dies." *New York Times*, March 3, 2008. http://www.nytimes. com/2008/03/03/business/03juran.html?_r=0.

Edison, Thomas A. *Diary and Sundry Observations of Thomas Alva Edison.* Edited by Dagobert D. Runes. New York: Greenwood Press, 1968.

Eisenhower, Dwight D. *At Ease: Stories I Tell My Friends.* New York: Doubleday, 1967.

Edgar F. Puryear Jr. *Nineteen Stars: A ensuring Study in Military Character and Leadership.* New York: Presidio Press, 1971.

Eisenhower, Dwight D. "Remarks at the National Defense Executive Reserve." November 14, 1957. Accessed August 15, 2013. http://www.eisenhower.archives.gov/all_about_ike/ quotes.html.

Eisenhower, Dwight D. "Remarks to Participants in the Young Republican National Leadership Training School." January 20, 1960. Accessed August 15, 2013. http://www.eisenhower. archives.gov/all_about_ike/quotes.html.

Gonzalez, Antonio. "We Should Have Won That Game." *Huffington Post*, February 5, 2013. Accessed February 12, 2013. http://www.huffingtonpost.com/2013/02/05/colin-kaepernick-49ers-super-bowl-should-have-won_n_2626061. html.

Gracian, Baltasar. *The Art of Worldly Wisdom*. Translated by Christopher Maurer. New York: Doubleday, 1991.

Johnson, Spencer, MD. *Who Moved My Cheese?* New York: G.P. Putnam's Sons, 1998.

"Justice Louis D. Brandeis." *Louis D. Brandeis Legacy Fund for Social Justice.* Accessed Dec 17, 2012. http://www.brandeis.edu/legacyfund/bio.html.

Katzenbach, Jon R. and Douglas K. Smith. *The Wisdom of Teams.* New York: Harvard Business School Press, 1993.

Kennedy, John F. "Annual Message to the Congress on the State of the Union." January 11, 1962. Accessed March 26, 2013. http://www.jfklibrary.org/Research/Research-Aids/Ready-Reference/JFK-Quotations.aspx.

Kotter, John and Holger Rathgeber. *Our Iceberg Is Melting.* New York: St. Martin's Press, 2006.

Lewis, Hedwig. *Body Language: A Guide for Professionals.* New Delhi: Response Books, 1998.

Lewis, James P. *Fundamentals of Project Management.* New York: AMACON, 1997.

Machiavelli, Niccolo. *The Prince.* Translated by Ninian Hill Thoamson, MA. New York: Franklin Watts, n.d.

McCullough, David G. *John Adams.* New York: Simon & Schuster, 2001.

Megginson, Leon C. "Lessons from Europe for American Business." *Southwestern Social Science Quarterly* 44, no. 1 (1963): 3-13.

Morris, Edmund. *The Rise of Theodore Roosevelt.* New York: Ballantine Books, 1979.

Shaw, George Bernard. "The Single Biggest Problem." *BrainyQuote. com.* Accessed January 16, 2013. http://www.brainyquote.com/quotes/quotes/g/georgebern385438.html.

INDEX